50 Southern Comfort Recipes for Home

By: Kelly Johnson

Table of Contents

- Shrimp and Grits
- Chicken and Waffles
- Biscuits and Gravy
- Fried Chicken
- Collard Greens
- Jambalaya
- Gumbo
- Red Beans and Rice
- Hushpuppies
- Cornbread
- Pecan Pie
- Key Lime Pie
- Banana Pudding
- Peach Cobbler
- Sweet Potato Pie
- Chicken Pot Pie
- Sausage Gravy
- Catfish Fry
- Southern Style Ribs
- Buttermilk Pancakes
- Fried Green Tomatoes
- Classic Mac and Cheese
- Baked Beans
- Deviled Eggs
- Southern Fried Okra
- Chicken and Dumplings
- BBQ Pulled Pork
- Cheese Grits
- Chicken Fried Steak
- Southern Corn Chowder
- Biscuits and Sausage Gravy Casserole
- Sweet Tea
- Country Ham
- Sautéed Kale
- Cucumber and Tomato Salad
- Fried Catfish Tacos

- Smothered Pork Chops
- Sloppy Joes
- Corn Pudding
- Broccoli and Cheese Casserole
- Southern Shrimp Salad
- Cajun Dirty Rice
- Hot Water Cornbread
- Apple Butter
- Poppy Seed Chicken
- Southern Cornbread Dressing
- Grits Casserole
- Hoppin' John
- Boiled Peanuts
- Cherry Limeade

Shrimp and Grits

Ingredients:

For the Grits:

- 1 cup stone-ground grits
- 4 cups water
- 1 cup milk
- 1/2 cup shredded sharp cheddar cheese
- 2 tablespoons butter
- Salt and pepper to taste

For the Shrimp:

- 1 pound large shrimp, peeled and deveined
- 2 tablespoons olive oil
- 4 slices bacon, chopped
- 1 bell pepper, diced
- 1 small onion, diced
- 3 cloves garlic, minced
- 1 cup chicken broth
- 1 tablespoon lemon juice
- 1 teaspoon smoked paprika
- 1/2 teaspoon cayenne pepper (optional, for extra heat)
- Salt and pepper to taste
- Chopped parsley for garnish

Instructions:

1. Prepare the Grits:

1. In a large saucepan, bring water to a boil.
2. Stir in grits and reduce heat to low. Cook, stirring occasionally, for 20-25 minutes or until grits are tender.
3. Stir in milk, cheese, and butter. Season with salt and pepper. Keep warm.

2. Cook the Shrimp:

1. Heat olive oil in a large skillet over medium heat.
2. Add chopped bacon and cook until crispy. Remove bacon with a slotted spoon and set aside, leaving the drippings in the skillet.
3. In the same skillet, add bell pepper and onion. Cook until softened, about 5 minutes.
4. Add garlic and cook for another minute.
5. Add shrimp to the skillet and cook until pink and opaque, about 2-3 minutes per side.

6. Pour in chicken broth, lemon juice, smoked paprika, cayenne pepper (if using), and season with salt and pepper. Cook until the sauce has slightly reduced, about 2-3 minutes.
7. Stir in the cooked bacon.

3. Assemble the Dish:

1. Spoon a portion of grits onto each plate.
2. Top with the shrimp mixture and spoon some of the sauce over the top.
3. Garnish with chopped parsley.

Serve and Enjoy!

Feel free to adjust the seasoning to your taste and add your favorite toppings.

Chicken and Waffles

Ingredients:

For the Chicken:

- 1 pound chicken wings or drumsticks
- 1 cup buttermilk
- 1 cup all-purpose flour
- 1 tablespoon paprika
- 1 teaspoon garlic powder
- 1 teaspoon onion powder
- 1/2 teaspoon cayenne pepper (optional)
- Salt and pepper to taste
- Vegetable oil for frying

For the Waffles:

- 2 cups all-purpose flour
- 2 tablespoons sugar
- 1 tablespoon baking powder
- 1/2 teaspoon salt
- 2 large eggs
- 1 3/4 cups milk
- 1/2 cup vegetable oil or melted butter
- 1 teaspoon vanilla extract

For Serving:

- Maple syrup
- Butter
- Optional: hot sauce, honey, or fruit preserves

Instructions:

1. Prepare the Chicken:

1. In a large bowl, marinate the chicken in buttermilk for at least 1 hour, or overnight in the refrigerator.
2. In a separate bowl, mix flour, paprika, garlic powder, onion powder, cayenne pepper, salt, and pepper.
3. Heat vegetable oil in a large skillet or deep fryer to 350°F (175°C).
4. Remove chicken from the buttermilk, allowing excess to drip off, and dredge in the seasoned flour mixture, coating thoroughly.

5. Fry chicken in batches until golden brown and cooked through, about 8-10 minutes per batch. Drain on paper towels and keep warm.

2. Make the Waffles:

1. Preheat your waffle iron according to the manufacturer's instructions.
2. In a large bowl, whisk together flour, sugar, baking powder, and salt.
3. In another bowl, beat eggs and then add milk, vegetable oil (or melted butter), and vanilla extract.
4. Pour the wet ingredients into the dry ingredients and stir until just combined (a few lumps are okay).
5. Lightly grease the waffle iron and pour batter onto the hot iron. Cook according to the manufacturer's instructions until waffles are golden brown and crispy.
6. Keep waffles warm in a low oven while you cook the remaining batter.

3. Assemble the Dish:

1. Place a waffle on each plate and top with a few pieces of fried chicken.
2. Drizzle with maple syrup and add a pat of butter if desired.
3. Optional: Serve with hot sauce, honey, or fruit preserves for extra flavor.

Serve and Enjoy!

This dish is a delightful combination of savory and sweet, perfect for breakfast, brunch, or even dinner.

Biscuits and Gravy

Ingredients:

For the Biscuits:

- 2 cups all-purpose flour
- 1 tablespoon baking powder
- 1/2 teaspoon baking soda
- 1/2 teaspoon salt
- 1/2 cup cold unsalted butter, cubed
- 1 cup buttermilk (more if needed)

For the Gravy:

- 1/2 pound breakfast sausage (bulk sausage, not in casings)
- 1/4 cup all-purpose flour
- 2 cups milk
- 1/2 teaspoon black pepper
- 1/4 teaspoon salt (or to taste)
- Optional: a pinch of cayenne pepper or red pepper flakes for heat

Instructions:

1. Make the Biscuits:

1. **Preheat the Oven:** Preheat your oven to 450°F (230°C).
2. **Mix Dry Ingredients:** In a large bowl, whisk together flour, baking powder, baking soda, and salt.
3. **Cut in the Butter:** Using a pastry cutter or your fingers, cut the cold butter into the flour mixture until it resembles coarse crumbs.
4. **Add Buttermilk:** Pour in the buttermilk and stir until just combined. The dough will be sticky.
5. **Roll and Cut:** Turn the dough onto a floured surface and gently knead a few times. Pat the dough to about 1-inch thickness and cut out biscuits using a round cutter or a glass.
6. **Bake:** Place biscuits on a baking sheet close together (for soft sides) or spaced apart (for crispy sides). Bake for 10-12 minutes, or until golden brown. Keep warm.

2. Make the Gravy:

1. **Cook the Sausage:** In a large skillet over medium heat, cook the sausage, breaking it up with a spoon until browned and cooked through. Remove the sausage with a slotted spoon and set aside, leaving the fat in the skillet.
2. **Make the Roux:** Sprinkle the flour over the sausage drippings in the skillet and stir to combine. Cook for about 1-2 minutes until the flour is lightly browned.

3. **Add Milk:** Gradually whisk in the milk, making sure there are no lumps. Continue to cook, stirring constantly, until the gravy thickens, about 5-7 minutes.
4. **Season:** Stir in the cooked sausage and season with black pepper and salt. Add a pinch of cayenne pepper or red pepper flakes if desired. Simmer for a few more minutes to meld the flavors.

3. Assemble and Serve:

1. **Serve:** Split the warm biscuits and ladle the sausage gravy over the top.
2. **Enjoy:** Serve immediately while the biscuits and gravy are hot.

Tips:

- For extra-flaky biscuits, avoid overworking the dough.
- Use a light touch when mixing and cutting out the biscuits to keep them tender.

Enjoy your delicious Biscuits and Gravy!

Fried Chicken

Ingredients:

For the Chicken:

- 3-4 pounds chicken pieces (legs, thighs, breasts, or a mix)
- 2 cups buttermilk
- 2 cups all-purpose flour
- 1 tablespoon paprika
- 1 teaspoon garlic powder
- 1 teaspoon onion powder
- 1 teaspoon dried thyme
- 1 teaspoon dried oregano
- 1/2 teaspoon cayenne pepper (optional, for heat)
- Salt and black pepper to taste
- Vegetable oil or peanut oil for frying

Instructions:

1. Marinate the Chicken:

1. **Marinate:** Place chicken pieces in a large bowl or zip-top bag. Pour buttermilk over the chicken, making sure all pieces are coated. Cover and refrigerate for at least 1 hour, or overnight for best results.

2. Prepare the Coating:

1. **Mix Dry Ingredients:** In a large bowl, whisk together flour, paprika, garlic powder, onion powder, dried thyme, dried oregano, cayenne pepper (if using), salt, and black pepper.

3. Coat the Chicken:

1. **Dredge Chicken:** Remove chicken from the buttermilk, allowing excess to drip off. Dredge each piece in the seasoned flour mixture, pressing lightly to adhere. For extra crispy chicken, double coat by dipping the floured chicken back into the buttermilk and then into the flour mixture again.

4. Fry the Chicken:

1. **Heat Oil:** In a large, heavy-bottomed skillet or deep fryer, heat about 1-2 inches of oil to 350°F (175°C). Use a thermometer to ensure the oil is at the correct temperature.
2. **Fry Chicken:** Carefully add chicken pieces to the hot oil, working in batches if necessary to avoid overcrowding. Fry for 8-12 minutes per side, or until the chicken is golden brown and the internal temperature reaches 165°F (74°C). Adjust heat as needed to maintain oil temperature.

3. **Drain:** Remove chicken from the oil and drain on a wire rack set over a baking sheet or on paper towels.

5. Serve:

1. **Rest:** Allow the chicken to rest for a few minutes before serving. This helps the juices redistribute and keeps the coating crispy.

Tips:

- Ensure the oil temperature remains consistent for even cooking.
- For a spicier version, adjust the amount of cayenne pepper or add hot sauce to the buttermilk marinade.

Enjoy your crispy, golden fried chicken!

Collard Greens

Ingredients:

- 2 bunches collard greens (about 2 pounds)
- 4 cups chicken or vegetable broth
- 1 smoked ham hock or 4 slices of bacon (optional for added flavor)
- 1 onion, finely chopped
- 3 cloves garlic, minced
- 1 tablespoon olive oil
- 1 teaspoon apple cider vinegar
- 1 teaspoon sugar (optional)
- Salt and black pepper to taste
- Red pepper flakes (optional, for heat)

Instructions:

1. Prepare the Collard Greens:

1. **Wash and Clean:** Rinse the collard greens thoroughly under cold water to remove any dirt or grit.
2. **Remove Stems:** Cut out the thick stems from the collard greens. Stack several leaves on top of each other, roll them up, and slice into strips (chiffonade).

2. Cook the Collard Greens:

1. **Sauté Aromatics:** In a large pot or Dutch oven, heat olive oil over medium heat. Add the chopped onion and cook until softened, about 5 minutes. Add the minced garlic and cook for another 1-2 minutes until fragrant.
2. **Add Broth and Meat:** Pour in the chicken or vegetable broth. If using, add the smoked ham hock or bacon for extra flavor. Bring to a simmer.
3. **Cook Greens:** Add the collard greens in batches, stirring to ensure they wilt down and are evenly coated with the broth. Once all the greens are added, cover the pot and reduce the heat to low. Simmer for 45-60 minutes, or until the greens are tender and flavorful. Stir occasionally.
4. **Season:** Remove the ham hock or bacon if used. Stir in apple cider vinegar, and sugar (if desired), and season with salt, black pepper, and red pepper flakes to taste. Adjust seasoning as needed.

3. Serve:

1. **Enjoy:** Serve collard greens hot as a side dish with your favorite Southern meal.

Tips:

- For a vegetarian version, omit the ham hock or bacon and use vegetable broth.
- Collard greens can be cooked ahead and stored in the refrigerator for up to 5 days. They often taste even better the next day as the flavors meld.

Enjoy your flavorful and hearty collard greens!

Jambalaya

Ingredients:

- 1 tablespoon olive oil
- 1 pound smoked sausage (like Andouille), sliced into 1/4-inch rounds
- 1 pound chicken thighs, boneless and skinless, cut into bite-sized pieces
- 1 large onion, chopped
- 1 bell pepper, chopped (red, green, or a mix)
- 3 cloves garlic, minced
- 1 can (14.5 oz) diced tomatoes
- 1 cup long-grain white rice
- 2 cups chicken broth
- 2 bay leaves
- 1 teaspoon dried thyme
- 1 teaspoon paprika
- 1/2 teaspoon cayenne pepper (optional, for heat)
- 1/2 teaspoon ground black pepper
- 1/2 teaspoon salt (or to taste)
- 1 pound large shrimp, peeled and deveined
- 2 green onions, sliced (for garnish)
- Fresh parsley, chopped (for garnish)

Instructions:

1. Cook the Sausage and Chicken:

1. **Heat Oil:** In a large pot or Dutch oven, heat olive oil over medium heat.
2. **Brown Sausage:** Add the sliced sausage and cook until browned. Remove the sausage from the pot and set aside.
3. **Cook Chicken:** In the same pot, add the chicken pieces. Cook until browned on all sides and cooked through. Remove the chicken from the pot and set aside with the sausage.

2. Sauté Vegetables:

1. **Cook Vegetables:** In the same pot, add the chopped onion and bell pepper. Sauté until the vegetables are softened, about 5 minutes.
2. **Add Garlic:** Stir in the minced garlic and cook for another minute until fragrant.

3. Add Rice and Seasonings:

1. **Combine Ingredients:** Add the rice to the pot and stir to coat with the vegetables.
2. **Add Tomatoes and Broth:** Stir in the diced tomatoes (with their juices) and chicken broth. Add bay leaves, dried thyme, paprika, cayenne pepper (if using), black pepper, and salt. Stir to combine.

4. Simmer:

1. **Simmer Rice:** Bring the mixture to a boil, then reduce the heat to low. Cover and simmer for 15-20 minutes, or until the rice is cooked and has absorbed most of the liquid.

5. Add Shrimp and Finish:

1. **Add Shrimp:** Stir in the shrimp and cooked sausage and chicken. Cover and cook for an additional 5-7 minutes, or until the shrimp are pink and cooked through.
2. **Garnish:** Remove the bay leaves. Garnish with sliced green onions and chopped fresh parsley.

Serve:

1. **Serve:** Spoon the jambalaya into bowls and enjoy!

Tips:

- For a spicier jambalaya, increase the amount of cayenne pepper or add hot sauce.
- You can customize the protein by adding other ingredients like crab, crawfish, or additional vegetables.

Enjoy your hearty and flavorful jambalaya!

Gumbo

Ingredients:

For the Gumbo:

- 1/2 cup vegetable oil
- 1/2 cup all-purpose flour
- 1 large onion, finely chopped
- 1 bell pepper, finely chopped (red or green)
- 3 cloves garlic, minced
- 2 celery stalks, finely chopped
- 1 pound smoked sausage (Andouille or similar), sliced into 1/4-inch rounds
- 1 pound chicken thighs, boneless and skinless, cut into bite-sized pieces
- 1 can (14.5 oz) diced tomatoes
- 4 cups chicken broth
- 1 bay leaf
- 1 teaspoon dried thyme
- 1 teaspoon paprika
- 1/2 teaspoon cayenne pepper (optional, for heat)
- 1/2 teaspoon ground black pepper
- 1 teaspoon salt (or to taste)
- 1 pound shrimp, peeled and deveined
- 1 cup frozen okra (or fresh if available), sliced
- 2 tablespoons chopped fresh parsley
- 4 green onions, sliced

For Serving:

- Cooked white rice
- File powder (optional, for added flavor)

Instructions:

1. Make the Roux:

1. **Heat Oil and Flour:** In a large pot or Dutch oven, heat vegetable oil over medium heat. Gradually whisk in flour, stirring constantly to make a roux.
2. **Cook Roux:** Continue to cook, stirring constantly, until the roux turns a deep brown color (like chocolate), about 15-20 minutes. Be careful not to burn it.

2. Sauté Vegetables:

1. **Add Vegetables:** Once the roux is ready, add the chopped onion, bell pepper, garlic, and celery. Cook until the vegetables are softened, about 5 minutes.

3. Add Meats and Broth:

1. **Cook Sausage and Chicken:** Add the sliced sausage and chicken pieces to the pot. Cook for a few minutes, stirring to combine.

2. **Add Tomatoes and Broth:** Stir in the diced tomatoes and chicken broth. Add bay leaf, dried thyme, paprika, cayenne pepper (if using), black pepper, and salt. Stir to combine.

4. Simmer:

1. **Simmer Gumbo:** Bring the mixture to a boil, then reduce heat to low. Cover and simmer for 30 minutes, stirring occasionally.

5. Add Shrimp and Okra:

1. **Add Okra and Shrimp:** Stir in the shrimp and okra. Cover and cook for an additional 5-7 minutes, or until the shrimp are pink and cooked through, and the okra is tender.

6. Finish and Serve:

1. **Garnish:** Stir in chopped parsley and sliced green onions. Adjust seasoning with additional salt and pepper if needed.
2. **Serve:** Ladle the gumbo over cooked white rice in bowls. Optionally, sprinkle with file powder for extra flavor.

Tips:

- **Roux:** The roux is a crucial component of gumbo, so be patient while cooking it to the right color.
- **Seafood Variation:** You can add other seafood like crab or crawfish if desired.
- **Okra:** Okra adds thickness and flavor, but it can be omitted if you prefer.

Enjoy your rich, flavorful gumbo!

Red Beans and Rice

Ingredients:

For the Red Beans:

- 1 pound dried red beans (or 2 cans, drained and rinsed)
- 1 tablespoon olive oil
- 1 large onion, chopped
- 1 bell pepper, chopped (red or green)
- 3 cloves garlic, minced
- 2 celery stalks, chopped
- 1 pound smoked sausage (Andouille or similar), sliced into 1/4-inch rounds
- 1 pound ham hock or 2 cups diced ham
- 4 cups chicken broth
- 1 can (14.5 oz) diced tomatoes
- 2 bay leaves
- 1 teaspoon dried thyme
- 1 teaspoon paprika
- 1/2 teaspoon cayenne pepper (optional, for heat)
- 1/2 teaspoon black pepper
- 1 teaspoon salt (or to taste)
- 2 tablespoons chopped fresh parsley
- 4 green onions, sliced (for garnish)

For Serving:

- Cooked white rice
- Hot sauce (optional, for serving)

Instructions:

1. Prepare the Beans:

1. **Soak Beans:** If using dried beans, rinse them and soak them overnight in plenty of water. Drain and rinse before cooking. (If using canned beans, skip this step.)

2. Cook the Red Beans:

1. **Sauté Vegetables:** In a large pot or Dutch oven, heat olive oil over medium heat. Add the chopped onion, bell pepper, garlic, and celery. Cook until softened, about 5 minutes.
2. **Add Sausage and Ham:** Stir in the sliced sausage and diced ham (or ham hock). Cook for a few minutes, until the sausage starts to brown.
3. **Add Beans and Broth:** Add the soaked (or canned) beans, chicken broth, diced tomatoes, bay leaves, dried thyme, paprika, cayenne pepper (if using), black pepper, and salt. Stir to combine.
4. **Simmer:** Bring to a boil, then reduce heat to low. Cover and simmer for 1.5 to 2 hours, or until the beans are tender and the flavors are well combined. If using canned beans, simmer for 30-45 minutes.

3. Mash Beans (Optional):

1. **Mash for Thickness:** For a thicker consistency, use a potato masher or the back of a spoon to mash some of the beans against the side of the pot. You can also use an immersion blender to blend a portion of the beans.

4. Finish and Serve:

1. **Garnish:** Stir in chopped parsley and adjust seasoning with additional salt and pepper if needed.
2. **Serve:** Serve the red beans over cooked white rice and garnish with sliced green onions. Add hot sauce to taste if desired.

Tips:

- **Flavor Development:** The dish often tastes even better the next day as the flavors meld.
- **Vegetarian Option:** You can omit the sausage and ham and use vegetable broth for a vegetarian version. Add smoked paprika to mimic some of the smoky flavors.

Enjoy your hearty and flavorful Red Beans and Rice!

Hushpuppies

Ingredients:

- 1 cup cornmeal
- 1/2 cup all-purpose flour
- 1 tablespoon sugar

- 1 tablespoon baking powder
- 1/2 teaspoon baking soda
- 1/2 teaspoon salt
- 1/4 teaspoon black pepper
- 1/2 cup finely chopped onion (optional: green onions for a milder flavor)
- 1/2 cup buttermilk
- 1 large egg
- Vegetable oil for frying

Instructions:

1. Prepare the Batter:

1. **Mix Dry Ingredients:** In a large bowl, combine cornmeal, flour, sugar, baking powder, baking soda, salt, and black pepper.
2. **Add Onion:** Stir in the finely chopped onion if using.
3. **Combine Wet Ingredients:** In a separate bowl, whisk together buttermilk and egg.
4. **Mix Batter:** Pour the wet ingredients into the dry ingredients and stir until just combined. The batter will be thick.

2. Heat Oil:

1. **Preheat Oil:** In a deep skillet or a large pot, heat about 2 inches of vegetable oil to 350°F (175°C). Use a thermometer to monitor the temperature.

3. Fry the Hushpuppies:

1. **Drop Batter:** Using a small scoop or spoon, carefully drop spoonfuls of the batter into the hot oil. Do not overcrowd the pan; work in batches if necessary.
2. **Fry Until Golden:** Fry the hushpuppies for about 2-3 minutes, or until they are golden brown and cooked through. They should float to the top when done.
3. **Drain:** Remove the hushpuppies with a slotted spoon and drain on paper towels.

4. Serve:

1. **Serve Warm:** Serve the hushpuppies warm as a side dish or appetizer. They are great with fried fish, shrimp, or other Southern dishes.

Tips:

- **Consistency:** If the batter is too thick to drop easily, add a little more buttermilk to reach the desired consistency.
- **Flavor Variations:** You can add additional ingredients like chopped jalapeños, shredded cheese, or herbs to the batter for different flavors.

Enjoy your crispy and delicious hushpuppies!

Cornbread

Ingredients:

- 1 cup cornmeal
- 1 cup all-purpose flour
- 1/4 cup granulated sugar (adjust to taste)
- 1 tablespoon baking powder

- 1/2 teaspoon salt
- 1 cup milk
- 2 large eggs
- 1/4 cup melted butter or vegetable oil

Instructions:

1. Preheat the Oven:

1. **Preheat Oven:** Preheat your oven to 425°F (220°C). Place a 9-inch round skillet or an 8-inch square baking pan in the oven while it heats.

2. Mix Dry Ingredients:

1. **Combine Dry Ingredients:** In a large bowl, whisk together cornmeal, flour, sugar, baking powder, and salt.

3. Mix Wet Ingredients:

1. **Combine Wet Ingredients:** In another bowl, whisk together milk, eggs, and melted butter (or oil).

4. Combine and Pour:

1. **Mix Batter:** Pour the wet ingredients into the dry ingredients and stir until just combined. The batter will be lumpy, and that's okay—do not overmix.
2. **Pour Batter:** Carefully remove the hot skillet or baking pan from the oven. Grease the pan lightly with butter or oil if not already seasoned. Pour the batter into the hot pan and spread it out evenly.

5. Bake:

1. **Bake:** Bake in the preheated oven for 20-25 minutes, or until the cornbread is golden brown and a toothpick inserted into the center comes out clean.

6. Serve:

1. **Cool Slightly:** Let the cornbread cool in the pan for a few minutes before cutting it into squares or wedges.
2. **Serve Warm:** Serve warm with butter, honey, or your favorite spread.

Tips:

- **For Extra Flavor:** You can add ingredients like shredded cheese, chopped jalapeños, or cooked bacon to the batter.

- **For Moist Cornbread:** If you prefer a moister cornbread, consider adding an extra tablespoon of melted butter or a dollop of sour cream to the batter.

Enjoy your homemade cornbread with your favorite Southern dishes or as a tasty standalone treat!

Pecan Pie

Here's a classic recipe for Pecan Pie:

Ingredients:

For the Pie Crust:

- 1 1/4 cups all-purpose flour
- 1/4 teaspoon salt
- 1/2 cup (1 stick) unsalted butter, cold and cut into small cubes
- 1/4 cup granulated sugar
- 1/4 cup ice water (more if needed)

For the Filling:

- 1 cup light corn syrup
- 1 cup packed brown sugar
- 1/2 cup unsalted butter, melted
- 3 large eggs
- 1 1/2 teaspoons vanilla extract
- 1/4 teaspoon salt
- 1 1/2 cups pecan halves

Instructions:

1. Prepare the Pie Crust:

1. **Mix Dry Ingredients:** In a medium bowl, whisk together flour and salt.
2. **Cut in Butter:** Add the cold butter cubes to the flour mixture. Use a pastry cutter or your fingers to cut the butter into the flour until the mixture resembles coarse crumbs.
3. **Add Sugar and Water:** Stir in the sugar. Gradually add ice water, one tablespoon at a time, until the dough begins to come together.
4. **Form and Chill:** Gather the dough into a ball, flatten it into a disk, wrap it in plastic wrap, and refrigerate for at least 30 minutes.

2. Preheat the Oven:

1. **Preheat Oven:** Preheat your oven to 350°F (175°C).

3. Roll Out the Dough:

1. **Roll Out:** On a lightly floured surface, roll out the chilled dough to fit a 9-inch pie pan. Transfer the dough to the pie pan, trim the edges, and crimp as desired.

4. Prepare the Filling:

1. **Mix Filling:** In a large bowl, whisk together the corn syrup, brown sugar, melted butter, eggs, vanilla extract, and salt until smooth.
2. **Add Pecans:** Stir in the pecan halves.

5. Assemble and Bake:

1. **Pour Filling:** Pour the filling into the prepared pie crust.

2. **Bake:** Bake in the preheated oven for 50-60 minutes, or until the filling is set and the crust is golden brown. The center of the pie should be slightly jiggly but will firm up as it cools.

6. Cool and Serve:

1. **Cool:** Allow the pie to cool completely on a wire rack before slicing. This helps the filling set properly.
2. **Serve:** Serve as is, or with a dollop of whipped cream or a scoop of vanilla ice cream.

Tips:

- **Prevent Overbrowning:** If the crust starts to get too dark, cover the edges with aluminum foil to prevent burning.
- **Make Ahead:** Pecan pie can be made ahead of time and stored at room temperature for up to 2 days, or refrigerated for up to a week.

Enjoy your delicious and classic pecan pie!

Key Lime Pie

Ingredients:

For the Crust:

- 1 1/2 cups graham cracker crumbs (about 10-12 graham crackers, crushed)
- 1/4 cup granulated sugar
- 6 tablespoons unsalted butter, melted

For the Filling:

- 4 large egg yolks
- 1 can (14 ounces) sweetened condensed milk
- 1/2 cup freshly squeezed key lime juice (or regular lime juice if key limes are not available)
- 1 tablespoon grated lime zest (optional, for added flavor)

For the Whipped Cream (optional):

- 1 cup heavy cream
- 2 tablespoons powdered sugar
- 1 teaspoon vanilla extract

Instructions:

1. Prepare the Crust:

1. **Preheat Oven:** Preheat your oven to 350°F (175°C).
2. **Mix Crust Ingredients:** In a medium bowl, combine graham cracker crumbs, granulated sugar, and melted butter. Stir until the mixture resembles wet sand.
3. **Form the Crust:** Press the mixture firmly into the bottom and up the sides of a 9-inch pie pan to form an even crust.
4. **Bake:** Bake in the preheated oven for 8-10 minutes, or until the crust is golden brown. Remove from the oven and let it cool while you prepare the filling.

2. Prepare the Filling:

1. **Mix Filling:** In a large bowl, whisk together egg yolks, sweetened condensed milk, key lime juice, and lime zest (if using) until smooth and well combined.
2. **Pour Filling:** Pour the filling into the cooled graham cracker crust.

3. Bake:

1. **Bake:** Bake in the oven for 15-20 minutes, or until the filling is set and the edges are slightly puffed. The center should still have a slight jiggle.
2. **Cool:** Remove from the oven and let the pie cool to room temperature. Then refrigerate for at least 3 hours, or until well chilled and set.

4. Prepare the Whipped Cream (optional):

1. **Whip Cream:** In a medium bowl, beat heavy cream with an electric mixer until soft peaks form. Add powdered sugar and vanilla extract, and continue to beat until stiff peaks form.
2. **Top Pie:** Spread or pipe the whipped cream over the chilled pie before serving.

5. Serve:

1. **Serve:** Slice and serve chilled. Garnish with additional lime zest or lime slices if desired.

Tips:

- **Key Limes vs. Regular Limes:** If key limes are not available, regular limes work perfectly fine. The flavor will be slightly different but still delicious.
- **Pie Storage:** Key lime pie can be stored in the refrigerator for up to a week or frozen for up to 2 months. Thaw in the refrigerator before serving.

Enjoy your tangy, creamy Key Lime Pie!

Banana Pudding

Ingredients:

For the Pudding:

- 1/2 cup granulated sugar
- 1/3 cup cornstarch
- 1/8 teaspoon salt
- 3 1/2 cups whole milk
- 3 large egg yolks
- 2 tablespoons unsalted butter
- 1 teaspoon vanilla extract

For Assembly:

- 4-5 ripe bananas, sliced
- 1 box (12 ounces) vanilla wafers

For the Whipped Cream (optional):

- 1 cup heavy cream
- 2 tablespoons powdered sugar
- 1 teaspoon vanilla extract

Instructions:

1. Prepare the Pudding:

1. **Mix Dry Ingredients:** In a medium saucepan, whisk together sugar, cornstarch, and salt.
2. **Add Milk:** Gradually whisk in the milk until smooth and combined.
3. **Cook Mixture:** Place the saucepan over medium heat and cook, whisking constantly, until the mixture begins to thicken and comes to a gentle boil. This will take about 5-7 minutes.
4. **Temper the Egg Yolks:** In a small bowl, lightly beat the egg yolks. Gradually add about 1/2 cup of the hot milk mixture to the egg yolks, whisking constantly to temper them.
5. **Combine and Cook:** Slowly whisk the egg yolk mixture back into the saucepan with the remaining milk mixture. Continue to cook, whisking constantly, for another 2-3 minutes until the pudding is thickened.
6. **Finish Pudding:** Remove from heat and whisk in the butter and vanilla extract until smooth.

2. Assemble the Banana Pudding:

1. **Layer Ingredients:** In a large bowl or trifle dish, spread a layer of vanilla wafers on the bottom. Top with a layer of banana slices. Spoon some of the pudding over the bananas and wafers.
2. **Repeat Layers:** Repeat the layers until you've used up all the pudding, bananas, and wafers, ending with a layer of pudding on top.

3. Prepare Whipped Cream (Optional):

1. **Whip Cream:** In a medium bowl, beat heavy cream with an electric mixer until soft peaks form. Add powdered sugar and vanilla extract, and continue to beat until stiff peaks form.
2. **Top Pudding:** Spread or pipe the whipped cream over the top of the pudding.

4. Chill:

1. **Refrigerate:** Cover and refrigerate the banana pudding for at least 4 hours, or overnight, to allow the flavors to meld and the pudding to set.

Tips:

- **Banana Browning:** To prevent the bananas from browning too quickly, you can toss them with a little lemon juice before layering.
- **Texture:** For a smoother texture, you can use a fine mesh strainer to strain the pudding before layering.

Enjoy your creamy, delicious Banana Pudding!

Peach Cobbler

Ingredients:

For the Filling:

- 6 cups fresh peaches (about 6-8 peaches), peeled, pitted, and sliced
- 1 cup granulated sugar

- 1/4 cup light brown sugar, packed
- 1/4 cup all-purpose flour
- 1/4 teaspoon ground cinnamon
- 1/8 teaspoon ground nutmeg
- 1 tablespoon lemon juice
- 1/4 teaspoon salt

For the Topping:

- 1 cup all-purpose flour
- 1/2 cup granulated sugar
- 1/2 cup light brown sugar, packed
- 1 1/2 teaspoons baking powder
- 1/2 teaspoon baking soda
- 1/2 teaspoon salt
- 1/2 cup (1 stick) unsalted butter, cold and cut into small cubes
- 1/2 cup buttermilk (or regular milk with 1 tablespoon lemon juice or vinegar)

Instructions:

1. Prepare the Peach Filling:

1. **Preheat Oven:** Preheat your oven to 375°F (190°C).
2. **Mix Filling:** In a large bowl, combine sliced peaches, granulated sugar, brown sugar, flour, cinnamon, nutmeg, lemon juice, and salt. Toss to coat the peaches evenly.
3. **Transfer to Dish:** Pour the peach mixture into a 2-quart baking dish (or similar size) and spread it out evenly.

2. Prepare the Topping:

1. **Mix Dry Ingredients:** In a medium bowl, whisk together flour, granulated sugar, brown sugar, baking powder, baking soda, and salt.
2. **Cut in Butter:** Add the cold butter cubes to the flour mixture. Use a pastry cutter, fork, or your fingers to cut the butter into the flour until the mixture resembles coarse crumbs.
3. **Add Buttermilk:** Pour in the buttermilk and stir until just combined. The batter will be lumpy.

3. Assemble and Bake:

1. **Top the Peaches:** Drop spoonfuls of the topping over the peach filling. The topping does not need to cover the filling completely.
2. **Bake:** Bake in the preheated oven for 45-55 minutes, or until the topping is golden brown and a toothpick inserted into the topping comes out clean. The filling should be bubbling around the edges.

4. Serve:

1. **Cool Slightly:** Let the cobbler cool for a few minutes before serving. This helps the filling to set slightly.
2. **Serve Warm:** Serve warm on its own or with a scoop of vanilla ice cream or a dollop of whipped cream.

Tips:

- **Peach Preparation:** If using frozen peaches, thaw and drain them before using. You may need to adjust the sugar and flour if the peaches are very juicy.
- **Flavor Enhancements:** Add a pinch of ground ginger or allspice to the filling for extra flavor.

Enjoy your homemade Peach Cobbler, perfect for summer or any time you crave a comforting dessert!

Sweet Potato Pie

Ingredients:

For the Pie Crust:

- 1 1/4 cups all-purpose flour
- 1/4 teaspoon salt
- 1/2 cup (1 stick) unsalted butter, cold and cut into small cubes
- 1/4 cup granulated sugar

- 1/4 cup ice water (more if needed)

For the Filling:

- 2 cups mashed sweet potatoes (about 2 medium sweet potatoes)
- 1 cup granulated sugar
- 1/2 cup packed light brown sugar
- 1/2 cup evaporated milk
- 2 large eggs
- 1/4 cup unsalted butter, melted
- 1 teaspoon vanilla extract
- 1 teaspoon ground cinnamon
- 1/2 teaspoon ground nutmeg
- 1/4 teaspoon ground ginger
- 1/4 teaspoon salt

Instructions:

1. Prepare the Pie Crust:

1. **Preheat Oven:** Preheat your oven to 375°F (190°C).
2. **Mix Dry Ingredients:** In a medium bowl, whisk together flour and salt.
3. **Cut in Butter:** Add the cold butter cubes to the flour mixture. Use a pastry cutter, fork, or your fingers to cut the butter into the flour until the mixture resembles coarse crumbs.
4. **Add Sugar and Water:** Stir in the granulated sugar. Gradually add ice water, one tablespoon at a time, until the dough begins to come together.
5. **Form and Chill:** Gather the dough into a ball, flatten it into a disk, wrap it in plastic wrap, and refrigerate for at least 30 minutes.
6. **Roll Out Dough:** On a lightly floured surface, roll out the chilled dough to fit a 9-inch pie pan. Transfer the dough to the pie pan, trim the edges, and crimp as desired.

2. Prepare the Filling:

1. **Cook Sweet Potatoes:** If you haven't done so already, peel and cube the sweet potatoes. Boil or steam them until tender, then mash until smooth. Measure out 2 cups of mashed sweet potatoes.
2. **Mix Filling:** In a large bowl, combine the mashed sweet potatoes, granulated sugar, brown sugar, evaporated milk, eggs, melted butter, vanilla extract, cinnamon, nutmeg, ginger, and salt. Whisk until smooth and well combined.

3. Assemble and Bake:

1. **Pour Filling:** Pour the sweet potato filling into the prepared pie crust.

2. **Bake:** Bake in the preheated oven for 50-60 minutes, or until the filling is set and a knife inserted into the center comes out clean. The pie should be firm but slightly jiggly in the center.
3. **Cool:** Allow the pie to cool completely on a wire rack before serving. This helps the filling to set properly.

4. Serve:

1. **Serve:** Serve the pie as is, or with a dollop of whipped cream or a scoop of vanilla ice cream.

Tips:

- **Pie Crust:** For a flakier crust, you can use a store-bought pie crust or make one ahead of time and freeze it.
- **Spice Variations:** Adjust the spices according to your taste preference. Some people like a bit more cinnamon or nutmeg.

Enjoy your creamy, spiced Sweet Potato Pie!

Chicken Pot Pie

Ingredients:

For the Filling:

- 2 cups cooked chicken, diced (use rotisserie chicken or leftover chicken)
- 1 cup frozen peas and carrots (or fresh if you prefer)
- 1 cup diced potatoes (peeled and cubed)

- 1/2 cup diced onion
- 1/2 cup diced celery
- 1/4 cup unsalted butter
- 1/4 cup all-purpose flour
- 1 3/4 cups chicken broth
- 1/2 cup milk
- 1/2 teaspoon dried thyme
- 1/2 teaspoon dried rosemary
- 1/2 teaspoon garlic powder
- Salt and pepper, to taste

For the Crust:

- 1 package (14.1 ounces) refrigerated pie crusts (or homemade if preferred)
- 1 large egg, beaten (for egg wash, optional)

Instructions:

1. Prepare the Filling:

1. **Cook Vegetables:** In a large skillet or saucepan, melt the butter over medium heat. Add the diced onion and celery, and cook until softened, about 5 minutes. Add the diced potatoes and cook for another 5 minutes.
2. **Make Roux:** Stir in the flour and cook for 1-2 minutes to form a roux (this will thicken the filling).
3. **Add Liquids:** Gradually whisk in the chicken broth and milk. Continue to cook, stirring constantly, until the mixture thickens and starts to bubble.
4. **Add Chicken and Vegetables:** Stir in the cooked chicken, peas, and carrots. Add dried thyme, dried rosemary, garlic powder, salt, and pepper. Mix until well combined. Remove from heat and set aside.

2. Assemble the Pie:

1. **Preheat Oven:** Preheat your oven to 425°F (220°C).
2. **Prepare Pie Crusts:** Roll out one pie crust and fit it into a 9-inch pie pan. Trim the edges if needed.
3. **Add Filling:** Pour the chicken filling into the pie crust.
4. **Top with Second Crust:** Roll out the second pie crust and place it over the filling. Trim and crimp the edges to seal. Cut a few small slits in the top crust to allow steam to escape.
5. **Apply Egg Wash:** If desired, brush the top crust with the beaten egg for a golden finish.

3. Bake:

1. **Bake Pie:** Bake in the preheated oven for 30-35 minutes, or until the crust is golden brown and the filling is bubbling. If the crust starts to over-brown, cover the edges with aluminum foil to prevent burning.
2. **Cool Slightly:** Allow the pie to cool for about 10 minutes before serving. This helps the filling set and makes it easier to slice.

Tips:

- **Vegetables:** Feel free to add other vegetables like corn or green beans based on your preference.
- **Crust:** For a homemade crust, use your favorite recipe or try a combination of butter and shortening for flakiness.

Enjoy your homemade Chicken Pot Pie, a perfect meal for a cozy night in!

Sausage Gravy

Ingredients:

- 1 pound breakfast sausage (bulk, not in casings)
- 1/4 cup all-purpose flour
- 2 cups whole milk
- 1/2 teaspoon black pepper (or to taste)

- 1/2 teaspoon salt (or to taste)
- 1/4 teaspoon crushed red pepper flakes (optional, for heat)

Instructions:

1. Cook the Sausage:

1. **Brown Sausage:** In a large skillet, cook the sausage over medium heat, breaking it up with a wooden spoon as it cooks. Continue to cook until the sausage is browned and cooked through, about 5-7 minutes.
2. **Drain Excess Fat:** If there is excess fat, carefully drain some of it off, leaving about 2-3 tablespoons in the skillet.

2. Make the Gravy:

1. **Add Flour:** Sprinkle the flour over the cooked sausage in the skillet. Stir well to coat the sausage with the flour. Cook for about 1-2 minutes, stirring constantly. This forms a roux and helps thicken the gravy.
2. **Add Milk:** Gradually whisk in the milk, making sure to smooth out any lumps. Continue to cook, stirring constantly, until the mixture starts to thicken and comes to a gentle simmer. This should take about 5 minutes.
3. **Season:** Stir in the black pepper, salt, and red pepper flakes (if using). Taste and adjust the seasoning if necessary.

3. Serve:

1. **Serve Warm:** Serve the sausage gravy warm over freshly baked biscuits, toast, or even pancakes.

Tips:

- **Consistency:** If the gravy is too thick, you can thin it with a little more milk. If it's too thin, let it simmer a bit longer to thicken.
- **For Extra Flavor:** Consider adding a splash of hot sauce or a bit of garlic powder for additional flavor.

Enjoy your hearty and delicious Sausage Gravy!

Catfish Fry

Ingredients:

For the Catfish:

- 4 catfish fillets (about 1 pound total)
- 1 cup buttermilk

- 1 cup all-purpose flour
- 1 cup cornmeal
- 1 teaspoon paprika
- 1 teaspoon garlic powder
- 1 teaspoon onion powder
- 1/2 teaspoon cayenne pepper (adjust to taste)
- 1/2 teaspoon salt
- 1/2 teaspoon black pepper
- Vegetable oil for frying

Instructions:

1. Prepare the Catfish:

1. **Soak in Buttermilk:** Place the catfish fillets in a shallow dish and pour the buttermilk over them. Let the fillets soak for at least 15 minutes (or up to 2 hours) in the refrigerator. This helps tenderize the fish and adds flavor.

2. Prepare the Coating:

1. **Mix Dry Ingredients:** In a large bowl, combine the flour, cornmeal, paprika, garlic powder, onion powder, cayenne pepper, salt, and black pepper. Mix well.

3. Coat the Catfish:

1. **Dredge Fillets:** Remove the catfish fillets from the buttermilk, allowing any excess to drip off. Dredge each fillet in the flour and cornmeal mixture, pressing lightly to ensure an even coating. Shake off any excess coating.

4. Heat the Oil:

1. **Preheat Oil:** In a large skillet or deep fryer, heat about 1/2 inch of vegetable oil over medium-high heat until it reaches 350°F (175°C). You can test the oil by dropping in a small pinch of the coating mixture; it should sizzle and float to the top.

5. Fry the Catfish:

1. **Fry Fillets:** Carefully place the coated catfish fillets in the hot oil. Fry in batches if necessary, being careful not to overcrowd the pan. Cook for about 3-4 minutes per side, or until the fillets are golden brown and crispy, and the internal temperature reaches 145°F (63°C).
2. **Drain:** Use a slotted spoon or tongs to remove the fillets from the oil and drain them on a plate lined with paper towels.

6. Serve:

1. **Serve Hot:** Serve the fried catfish fillets hot with your favorite sides such as coleslaw, fries, or cornbread. You can also add a wedge of lemon and a side of tartar sauce or hot sauce for extra flavor.

Tips:

- **Oil Temperature:** Keep an eye on the oil temperature to ensure it stays around 350°F. Too hot, and the coating may burn before the fish cooks through; too cool, and the fish may absorb excess oil and become greasy.
- **Flavor Variations:** Adjust the seasoning in the coating to your taste, or try adding a bit of dried herbs like thyme or oregano for additional flavor.

Enjoy your crispy, golden-brown catfish!

Southern Style Ribs

Ingredients:

For the Ribs:

- 2 racks of pork baby back ribs (about 4-5 pounds total)
- 1 tablespoon olive oil

For the Dry Rub:

- 1/4 cup brown sugar
- 2 tablespoons paprika
- 1 tablespoon garlic powder
- 1 tablespoon onion powder
- 1 teaspoon cayenne pepper (adjust to taste)
- 1 teaspoon black pepper
- 1 teaspoon salt
- 1/2 teaspoon ground cumin
- 1/2 teaspoon dried thyme (optional)

For the BBQ Sauce (optional):

- 1 cup ketchup
- 1/2 cup apple cider vinegar
- 1/2 cup brown sugar
- 1/4 cup honey
- 2 tablespoons Worcestershire sauce
- 1 tablespoon lemon juice
- 1 teaspoon smoked paprika
- 1/2 teaspoon garlic powder
- 1/2 teaspoon onion powder
- Salt and pepper, to taste

Instructions:

1. Prepare the Ribs:

1. **Remove Membrane:** Place the ribs on a cutting board. Use a paper towel to grip the thin membrane on the back of the ribs and peel it off. This helps make the ribs more tender.
2. **Season Ribs:** Rub the ribs with olive oil on both sides. Generously apply the dry rub mixture to both sides of the ribs, pressing it in to adhere well.

2. Cook the Ribs:

1. **Preheat Oven:** Preheat your oven to 300°F (150°C).
2. **Wrap Ribs:** Place each rack of ribs on a large piece of aluminum foil, bone side down. Wrap tightly to form a sealed packet.
3. **Bake:** Place the wrapped ribs on a baking sheet and bake in the preheated oven for 2.5 to 3 hours, or until the ribs are tender. The meat should be pulling away from the bones.

3. Prepare the BBQ Sauce (Optional):

1. **Mix Sauce Ingredients:** In a medium saucepan, combine all BBQ sauce ingredients. Bring to a simmer over medium heat, stirring occasionally.
2. **Simmer:** Reduce heat and let the sauce simmer for about 15-20 minutes, until thickened. Adjust seasoning with salt and pepper to taste. Remove from heat.

4. Finish the Ribs:

1. **Preheat Grill:** Preheat your grill to medium-high heat (about 400°F or 200°C).
2. **Grill Ribs:** Remove the ribs from the foil and discard any excess juices. Brush the ribs with a layer of BBQ sauce (if using) and place them on the grill.
3. **Grill for Flavor:** Grill the ribs for about 5-7 minutes per side, or until you get a nice caramelized crust and grill marks. Brush with additional BBQ sauce as needed.

5. Serve:

1. **Rest Ribs:** Remove the ribs from the grill and let them rest for a few minutes before slicing.
2. **Serve:** Slice between the bones and serve with extra BBQ sauce on the side, if desired.

Tips:

- **For Extra Tender Ribs:** You can also cook the ribs in a slow cooker on low for 6-7 hours instead of baking. Finish them on the grill as described above for a great texture.
- **Flavor Variations:** Experiment with different spices in the dry rub or add a splash of bourbon or apple cider vinegar to the BBQ sauce for unique flavors.

Enjoy your flavorful Southern Style Ribs!

Buttermilk Pancakes

Ingredients:

- 1 1/2 cups all-purpose flour
- 2 tablespoons granulated sugar
- 1 tablespoon baking powder
- 1/2 teaspoon baking soda

- 1/2 teaspoon salt
- 1 1/4 cups buttermilk
- 1/4 cup whole milk
- 1 large egg
- 3 tablespoons unsalted butter, melted (plus extra for the pan)
- 1 teaspoon vanilla extract (optional)

Instructions:

1. Prepare the Dry Ingredients:

1. **Mix Dry Ingredients:** In a large bowl, whisk together the flour, sugar, baking powder, baking soda, and salt.

2. Prepare the Wet Ingredients:

1. **Combine Wet Ingredients:** In another bowl or large measuring cup, whisk together the buttermilk, whole milk, egg, melted butter, and vanilla extract (if using).

3. Mix Batter:

1. **Combine Wet and Dry Ingredients:** Pour the wet ingredients into the dry ingredients. Gently stir until just combined. The batter should be slightly lumpy—don't overmix. Overmixing can result in tough pancakes.

4. Cook the Pancakes:

1. **Preheat Pan or Griddle:** Heat a large nonstick skillet or griddle over medium heat. Lightly grease with a small amount of butter or cooking spray.
2. **Pour Batter:** For each pancake, pour about 1/4 cup of batter onto the hot pan. Use the back of a spoon or measuring cup to spread it out if needed.
3. **Cook Pancakes:** Cook until bubbles start to form on the surface and the edges look set, about 2-3 minutes. Flip and cook for another 1-2 minutes, or until golden brown and cooked through.

5. Serve:

1. **Serve Warm:** Transfer pancakes to a plate and keep warm while you cook the remaining pancakes. Serve with your favorite toppings such as maple syrup, fresh fruit, whipped cream, or butter.

Tips:

- **Consistency:** If the batter is too thick, you can add a little more milk to reach your desired consistency.

- **Keeping Pancakes Warm:** To keep pancakes warm while cooking the rest, place them on a baking sheet in a 200°F (90°C) oven.

Enjoy your homemade buttermilk pancakes, perfect for a delicious breakfast or bru

Fried Green Tomatoes

Ingredients:

- 4-5 medium green tomatoes
- 1 cup all-purpose flour
- 1 cup cornmeal

- 1 teaspoon paprika
- 1/2 teaspoon garlic powder
- 1/2 teaspoon onion powder
- 1/2 teaspoon cayenne pepper (optional, for heat)
- 1/2 teaspoon salt
- 1/2 teaspoon black pepper
- 2 large eggs
- 1/4 cup milk
- Vegetable oil for frying

Instructions:

1. Prepare the Tomatoes:

1. **Slice Tomatoes:** Wash and slice the green tomatoes into 1/4 to 1/2-inch thick slices. Arrange them on a paper towel and sprinkle lightly with salt. Let them sit for about 10 minutes to draw out excess moisture. Pat dry with additional paper towels.

2. Prepare the Coating:

1. **Mix Flour and Seasonings:** In a shallow dish, combine the flour, cornmeal, paprika, garlic powder, onion powder, cayenne pepper (if using), salt, and black pepper.
2. **Prepare Egg Mixture:** In another shallow dish, whisk together the eggs and milk.

3. Coat the Tomatoes:

1. **Dredge in Flour Mixture:** Dip each tomato slice into the flour mixture, coating both sides evenly.
2. **Dip in Egg Mixture:** Next, dip the coated tomato slice into the egg mixture, allowing any excess to drip off.
3. **Coat Again:** Return the slice to the flour mixture, pressing lightly to adhere a second layer of coating. Shake off any excess.

4. Fry the Tomatoes:

1. **Heat Oil:** In a large skillet or cast-iron pan, heat about 1/4 inch of vegetable oil over medium-high heat until it reaches 350°F (175°C). You can test the oil by dropping in a small pinch of the coating mixture; it should sizzle and float.
2. **Fry Slices:** Carefully place the tomato slices in the hot oil, working in batches if necessary to avoid overcrowding. Fry for about 2-3 minutes per side, or until golden brown and crispy.
3. **Drain:** Use a slotted spoon or tongs to remove the fried tomatoes from the skillet and place them on a plate lined with paper towels to drain any excess oil.

5. Serve:

1. **Serve Warm:** Serve the fried green tomatoes hot with your favorite dipping sauce, such as ranch dressing or a remoulade sauce. They can also be enjoyed on their own as a delicious snack or appetizer.

Tips:

- **Oil Temperature:** Keep the oil temperature consistent to ensure even cooking and avoid greasy tomatoes. Adjust the heat as needed.
- **Crispier Texture:** For extra crispiness, you can use panko breadcrumbs in addition to the cornmeal in the coating mixture.

Enjoy your crispy and tangy Fried Green Tomatoes!

Classic Mac and Cheese

Ingredients:

For the Pasta:

- 1 pound elbow macaroni (or your preferred pasta shape)
- Salt (for pasta water)

For the Cheese Sauce:

- 4 tablespoons unsalted butter
- 1/4 cup all-purpose flour
- 2 cups whole milk
- 1 cup heavy cream
- 2 cups shredded sharp cheddar cheese
- 1 cup shredded Gruyère or mozzarella cheese (optional, for extra creaminess)
- 1/2 teaspoon garlic powder
- 1/2 teaspoon onion powder
- 1/2 teaspoon mustard powder (optional, for added depth of flavor)
- Salt and black pepper to taste

For the Topping (optional):

- 1 cup panko breadcrumbs
- 2 tablespoons melted butter
- 1/4 cup grated Parmesan cheese

Instructions:

1. Cook the Pasta:

1. **Boil Pasta:** In a large pot, bring salted water to a boil. Cook the macaroni according to package instructions until al dente. Drain and set aside.

2. Make the Cheese Sauce:

1. **Melt Butter:** In a large saucepan or skillet, melt the butter over medium heat.
2. **Make Roux:** Whisk in the flour and cook for about 1-2 minutes, stirring constantly. This forms a roux, which will thicken the sauce.
3. **Add Milk and Cream:** Gradually whisk in the milk and heavy cream, making sure to smooth out any lumps. Continue to cook and whisk until the mixture starts to thicken and comes to a gentle simmer.
4. **Add Cheese:** Lower the heat to medium-low and add the shredded cheddar cheese and Gruyère (if using). Stir until the cheese is completely melted and the sauce is smooth.
5. **Season:** Stir in garlic powder, onion powder, mustard powder (if using), salt, and black pepper. Taste and adjust seasoning as needed.

3. Combine Pasta and Sauce:

1. **Mix Pasta and Sauce:** Add the cooked macaroni to the cheese sauce and stir until well coated.

4. Prepare the Topping (Optional):

1. **Mix Topping:** In a small bowl, combine the panko breadcrumbs, melted butter, and grated Parmesan cheese.

5. Bake (Optional):

1. **Preheat Oven:** Preheat your oven to 375°F (190°C).
2. **Transfer to Baking Dish:** Pour the mac and cheese into a greased 9x13-inch baking dish.
3. **Add Topping:** Sprinkle the breadcrumb mixture evenly over the top of the mac and cheese.
4. **Bake:** Bake in the preheated oven for 20-25 minutes, or until the top is golden brown and the sauce is bubbling.

6. Serve:

1. **Cool Slightly:** Allow the mac and cheese to cool for a few minutes before serving to let the sauce set.

Tips:

- **Cheese Choices:** Feel free to mix different cheeses for a more complex flavor. Fontina, Monterey Jack, or even a bit of blue cheese can add unique notes.
- **Creaminess:** For an extra creamy texture, you can add a splash of milk or cream if the sauce thickens too much while baking.

Enjoy your homemade Classic Mac and Cheese, perfect as a comforting side dish or a hearty main course!

Baked Beans

Ingredients:

- 4 cups dried navy beans (or 2 cans of navy beans, drained and rinsed)
- 1/2 pound bacon, diced
- 1 onion, finely chopped
- 1/2 cup packed brown sugar

- 1/4 cup molasses
- 1/4 cup ketchup
- 2 tablespoons Dijon mustard
- 1 tablespoon Worcestershire sauce
- 1/2 teaspoon smoked paprika (or regular paprika)
- 1/2 teaspoon ground black pepper
- 1/2 teaspoon salt
- 1/4 teaspoon ground black pepper
- 1/2 teaspoon garlic powder (optional)
- 1/4 teaspoon cayenne pepper (optional, for heat)

Instructions:

1. Prepare the Beans:

1. **Soak Beans:** If using dried beans, rinse them and place them in a large bowl. Cover with water and let soak overnight. Drain and rinse the beans. If you're short on time, you can use the quick soak method: Bring the beans and water to a boil, let boil for 2 minutes, then remove from heat, cover, and let sit for 1 hour. Drain and rinse.
2. **Cook Beans:** Place the soaked beans in a large pot, cover with fresh water, and bring to a boil. Reduce heat and simmer until tender but still firm, about 1 to 1.5 hours. Drain and set aside.

2. Prepare the Sauce:

1. **Cook Bacon:** In a large skillet, cook the diced bacon over medium heat until crisp. Remove the bacon with a slotted spoon and drain on paper towels. Leave about 2 tablespoons of bacon drippings in the skillet.
2. **Sauté Onion:** In the same skillet, add the chopped onion and cook until softened and translucent, about 5 minutes.

3. Combine Ingredients:

1. **Mix Sauce Ingredients:** In a large bowl, combine brown sugar, molasses, ketchup, Dijon mustard, Worcestershire sauce, smoked paprika, salt, black pepper, garlic powder (if using), and cayenne pepper (if using). Mix well.
2. **Combine Beans and Sauce:** Add the cooked beans, bacon, and sautéed onions to the bowl with the sauce mixture. Stir to coat the beans evenly.

4. Bake the Beans:

1. **Preheat Oven:** Preheat your oven to 325°F (165°C).
2. **Transfer to Baking Dish:** Pour the bean mixture into a greased 2-quart baking dish or a similar-sized oven-safe dish.

3. **Bake:** Bake in the preheated oven for 1.5 to 2 hours, stirring occasionally, until the beans are tender and the sauce is thickened. If the sauce starts to get too thick, you can add a bit of water or broth to loosen it.

5. Serve:

1. **Cool Slightly:** Let the baked beans cool for a few minutes before serving. This helps the flavors meld and makes them easier to serve.

Tips:

- **Beans:** If using canned beans, reduce the baking time as they are already cooked. Combine the beans with the sauce and bake for 30-45 minutes.
- **Variations:** Add a teaspoon of liquid smoke for a smoky flavor, or mix in some diced bell peppers for added texture and flavor.

Enjoy your homemade Baked Beans, perfect for complementing any meal!

Deviled Eggs

Ingredients:

- 6 large eggs
- 1/4 cup mayonnaise
- 1 teaspoon Dijon mustard

- 1 teaspoon white vinegar or apple cider vinegar
- 1/4 teaspoon salt
- 1/4 teaspoon black pepper
- Paprika (for garnish)
- Chopped fresh chives or parsley (optional, for garnish)

Instructions:

1. Cook the Eggs:

1. **Boil Eggs:** Place the eggs in a single layer in a saucepan. Cover with cold water, about 1 inch above the eggs. Bring to a boil over medium-high heat.
2. **Simmer:** Once boiling, reduce the heat to low and cover the pan. Let simmer for 9-12 minutes.
3. **Cool Eggs:** Remove the eggs from the hot water and transfer them to a bowl of ice water. Let them cool for about 5 minutes.

2. Peel and Prepare the Eggs:

1. **Peel Eggs:** Gently crack the eggshells and peel under running water to remove any small bits of shell.
2. **Slice Eggs:** Slice each egg in half lengthwise.

3. Prepare the Filling:

1. **Remove Yolks:** Carefully remove the yolks from the egg whites and place them in a medium bowl.
2. **Mix Filling:** Mash the yolks with a fork. Add mayonnaise, Dijon mustard, vinegar, salt, and black pepper. Mix until smooth and creamy. Adjust seasoning to taste if needed.

4. Assemble the Deviled Eggs:

1. **Fill Egg Whites:** Spoon or pipe the yolk mixture into the egg white halves. If using a piping bag, you can fit it with a star tip for a decorative touch.
2. **Garnish:** Sprinkle a little paprika on top for color and extra flavor. Garnish with chopped fresh chives or parsley if desired.

5. Serve:

1. **Chill:** Refrigerate the deviled eggs until ready to serve. They are best served chilled.

Tips:

- **Creamy Texture:** For extra creaminess, you can use a combination of mayonnaise and sour cream.

- **Variations:** Add a pinch of cayenne pepper or a splash of hot sauce to the yolk mixture for a spicy kick. You can also experiment with adding chopped pickles, relish, or crumbled bacon to the filling.

Enjoy your classic and delicious Deviled Eggs!

Southern Fried Okra

Ingredients:

- 1 pound fresh okra (or frozen, if fresh is unavailable)
- 1 cup buttermilk

- 1 cup all-purpose flour
- 1 cup cornmeal
- 1 teaspoon paprika
- 1/2 teaspoon garlic powder
- 1/2 teaspoon onion powder
- 1/2 teaspoon cayenne pepper (optional, for heat)
- 1/2 teaspoon salt
- 1/2 teaspoon black pepper
- Vegetable oil for frying

Instructions:

1. Prepare the Okra:

1. **Wash and Slice:** If using fresh okra, wash and pat dry. Slice the okra into 1/4-inch rounds. If using frozen okra, thaw and drain well, patting dry with paper towels to remove excess moisture.

2. Prepare the Coating:

1. **Soak in Buttermilk:** Place the okra slices in a bowl and pour the buttermilk over them. Stir to coat and let soak for about 15-20 minutes.
2. **Mix Coating Ingredients:** In a separate bowl, combine the flour, cornmeal, paprika, garlic powder, onion powder, cayenne pepper (if using), salt, and black pepper.

3. Coat the Okra:

1. **Dredge in Coating:** Remove a handful of okra slices from the buttermilk, letting any excess drip off. Dredge them in the flour and cornmeal mixture, ensuring they are evenly coated. Shake off any excess coating. Repeat with remaining okra slices.

4. Fry the Okra:

1. **Heat Oil:** In a large skillet or deep fryer, heat about 1/2 inch of vegetable oil over medium-high heat until it reaches 350°F (175°C). You can test the oil by dropping in a small pinch of the coating mixture; it should sizzle and float.
2. **Fry Okra:** Carefully place the coated okra slices in the hot oil, working in batches to avoid overcrowding. Fry for about 3-4 minutes, or until golden brown and crispy. Turn the okra occasionally for even cooking.
3. **Drain:** Use a slotted spoon to remove the fried okra from the oil and place them on a plate lined with paper towels to drain any excess oil.

5. Serve:

1. **Serve Hot:** Serve the fried okra hot, seasoned with a little extra salt if desired. They make a great side dish or snack on their own, or with a dipping sauce such as ranch dressing or hot sauce.

Tips:

- **Oil Temperature:** Keeping the oil at the right temperature is key to achieving crispy okra. Adjust the heat as needed to maintain 350°F.
- **For Extra Crispiness:** You can add a bit of baking powder to the flour and cornmeal mixture for extra crunch.

Enjoy your crispy and delicious Southern Fried Okra!

Chicken and Dumplings

Ingredients:

For the Chicken Stew:

- 2 tablespoons olive oil
- 1 medium onion, chopped
- 2 cloves garlic, minced
- 3 medium carrots, sliced
- 3 celery stalks, sliced
- 1 teaspoon dried thyme
- 1 teaspoon dried parsley
- 1/2 teaspoon dried rosemary
- 1/2 teaspoon salt (or to taste)
- 1/4 teaspoon black pepper (or to taste)
- 1/4 cup all-purpose flour
- 4 cups chicken broth
- 2 cups cooked chicken, shredded or diced (use rotisserie or leftover chicken)
- 1 cup frozen peas
- 1 cup heavy cream or whole milk

For the Dumplings:

- 2 cups all-purpose flour
- 2 tablespoons baking powder
- 1/2 teaspoon salt
- 1/4 teaspoon black pepper
- 1/4 cup unsalted butter, cold and cut into small pieces
- 3/4 cup milk

Instructions:

1. Prepare the Chicken Stew:

1. **Cook Vegetables:** In a large pot or Dutch oven, heat the olive oil over medium heat. Add the chopped onion, garlic, carrots, and celery. Cook until the vegetables are softened, about 5-7 minutes.
2. **Add Seasonings:** Stir in the thyme, parsley, rosemary, salt, and pepper.
3. **Make the Roux:** Sprinkle the flour over the vegetables and stir to coat. Cook for about 1-2 minutes to remove the raw flour taste.
4. **Add Broth and Chicken:** Gradually whisk in the chicken broth, making sure to smooth out any lumps. Stir in the cooked chicken.
5. **Simmer:** Bring the mixture to a simmer and cook for about 10 minutes, or until the vegetables are tender and the stew has thickened slightly.
6. **Add Cream:** Stir in the heavy cream or milk and frozen peas. Adjust seasoning if needed.

2. Prepare the Dumplings:

1. **Mix Dry Ingredients:** In a medium bowl, whisk together the flour, baking powder, salt, and black pepper.
2. **Cut in Butter:** Add the cold butter pieces and use a pastry cutter or your fingers to cut the butter into the flour mixture until it resembles coarse crumbs.
3. **Add Milk:** Pour in the milk and stir until just combined. The dough will be thick and lumpy.

3. Cook the Dumplings:

1. **Drop Dumplings:** Using a spoon, drop spoonfuls of the dumpling dough over the simmering chicken stew. Space them slightly apart. You should have enough dough to cover the surface of the stew with several dumplings.
2. **Cover and Cook:** Reduce the heat to low, cover the pot, and cook for about 15-20 minutes, or until the dumplings are cooked through and fluffy. Avoid lifting the lid during this time, as it may cause the dumplings to become dense.

4. Serve:

1. **Serve Hot:** Spoon the chicken and dumplings into bowls and serve hot.

Tips:

- **Dumpling Texture:** For lighter dumplings, be careful not to overmix the dough. It should be just combined.
- **Thicker Stew:** If the stew is too thick, you can add a bit more chicken broth or milk to reach your desired consistency.

Enjoy your hearty and comforting Chicken and Dumplings!

BBQ Pulled Pork

Ingredients:

For the Pork:

- 4-5 pounds pork shoulder (also known as pork butt)
- 2 tablespoons olive oil
- Salt and black pepper (to taste)

For the Dry Rub:

- 1/4 cup brown sugar
- 2 tablespoons paprika
- 1 tablespoon garlic powder
- 1 tablespoon onion powder
- 1 tablespoon chili powder
- 1 teaspoon cumin
- 1 teaspoon smoked paprika (optional, for extra smokiness)
- 1 teaspoon salt
- 1/2 teaspoon black pepper
- 1/2 teaspoon cayenne pepper (optional, for heat)

For the BBQ Sauce (optional, or use your favorite store-bought sauce):

- 1 cup ketchup
- 1/2 cup apple cider vinegar
- 1/2 cup brown sugar
- 1/4 cup honey
- 2 tablespoons Worcestershire sauce
- 1 tablespoon lemon juice
- 1 teaspoon smoked paprika
- 1/2 teaspoon garlic powder
- 1/2 teaspoon onion powder
- Salt and pepper to taste

Instructions:

1. Prepare the Pork:

1. **Season Pork:** Pat the pork shoulder dry with paper towels. Rub the pork all over with olive oil, then season generously with salt and black pepper.
2. **Apply Dry Rub:** In a small bowl, mix together all the dry rub ingredients. Rub the mixture all over the pork shoulder, covering it evenly.

2. Cook the Pork:

1. **Slow Cooker Method:**
    - **Transfer to Slow Cooker:** Place the seasoned pork shoulder in a slow cooker.

- **Cook:** Cover and cook on low for 8-10 hours, or until the pork is tender and easily shreds with a fork.
- **Shred:** Remove the pork from the slow cooker and place it on a large cutting board. Shred the pork using two forks, discarding any large pieces of fat. Return the shredded pork to the slow cooker and mix with the juices.

2. **Oven Method:**
    - **Preheat Oven:** Preheat your oven to 300°F (150°C).
    - **Roast Pork:** Place the seasoned pork shoulder in a roasting pan or on a rack in a baking dish. Cover tightly with aluminum foil.
    - **Cook:** Roast for 4-5 hours, or until the pork is tender and shreds easily with a fork.
    - **Shred:** Remove the pork from the oven and let it rest for a few minutes before shredding. Return the shredded pork to the pan, mixing with the pan juices.

3. Prepare the BBQ Sauce (if using homemade):

    1. **Combine Sauce Ingredients:** In a medium saucepan, combine all BBQ sauce ingredients. Bring to a simmer over medium heat, stirring occasionally.
    2. **Simmer:** Reduce heat and let the sauce simmer for 15-20 minutes, or until slightly thickened. Adjust seasoning with salt and pepper to taste.

4. Serve:

    1. **Mix with Sauce:** If desired, mix the shredded pork with BBQ sauce. You can add as much or as little as you prefer.
    2. **Serve:** Serve the pulled pork on sandwich buns with extra BBQ sauce on the side, or as a main dish with sides like coleslaw or baked beans.

Tips:

- **Resting Time:** Letting the pork rest after cooking allows the juices to redistribute, making the meat more flavorful and easier to shred.
- **Flavor Variations:** Experiment with different types of BBQ sauce or add a splash of apple cider vinegar to the pulled pork for extra tanginess.

Enjoy your flavorful and tender BBQ Pulled Pork!

Cheese Grits

Ingredients:

- 1 cup stone-ground grits
- 4 cups water (or you can use chicken or vegetable broth for more flavor)
- 1 teaspoon salt
- 2 tablespoons unsalted butter
- 1 cup shredded sharp cheddar cheese
- 1/2 cup milk or heavy cream
- 1/4 teaspoon black pepper (or to taste)
- 1/4 teaspoon garlic powder (optional)
- 1/4 teaspoon onion powder (optional)

Instructions:

1. Cook the Grits:

1. **Boil Water:** In a large pot, bring 4 cups of water (or broth) to a boil. Add 1 teaspoon of salt.
2. **Add Grits:** Gradually whisk in the grits to prevent lumps. Reduce heat to low and cover.
3. **Simmer:** Cook the grits, stirring occasionally, for about 20-25 minutes or until they are tender and have absorbed most of the liquid. Stone-ground grits may take a bit longer, so adjust cooking time as needed.

2. Finish the Grits:

1. **Add Butter and Cheese:** Once the grits are cooked and creamy, stir in the butter until melted and fully incorporated. Then add the shredded cheddar cheese and stir until the cheese is melted and the mixture is smooth.
2. **Add Milk/Cream:** Stir in the milk or heavy cream to achieve your desired consistency. If the grits are too thick, add more milk or cream until they reach the desired creaminess.
3. **Season:** Season with black pepper and, if desired, garlic powder and onion powder. Taste and adjust seasoning as needed.

3. Serve:

1. **Serve Warm:** Serve the cheese grits warm as a side dish. They pair wonderfully with fried chicken, shrimp and grits, or even as a hearty breakfast.

Tips:

- **Consistency:** If the grits become too thick after cooking, you can stir in a bit more milk or cream to loosen them up.
- **Cheese Variations:** For different flavors, you can use a mix of cheeses such as Monterey Jack, Gruyère, or Parmesan.
- **Make-Ahead:** Cheese grits can be made ahead and reheated. Add a little extra milk or cream when reheating to restore creaminess.

Enjoy your creamy and cheesy grits!

Chicken Fried Steak

Ingredients:

For the Steak:

- 4 beef cube steaks (about 4-6 ounces each)
- 1 cup all-purpose flour
- 1 teaspoon salt
- 1/2 teaspoon black pepper
- 1 teaspoon paprika
- 1/2 teaspoon garlic powder
- 1/2 teaspoon onion powder
- 2 large eggs
- 1 cup buttermilk
- Vegetable oil for frying

For the Gravy:

- 3 tablespoons all-purpose flour (for gravy)
- 2 cups milk
- 1/2 cup chicken broth (or beef broth)
- Salt and black pepper to taste

Instructions:

1. Prepare the Steaks:

1. **Tenderize:** If the cube steaks are not already tenderized, use a meat mallet to pound them to about 1/2 inch thickness.
2. **Season:** Season the steaks with salt and black pepper on both sides.

2. Prepare the Breading:

1. **Mix Flour and Seasonings:** In a shallow dish, combine 1 cup of flour, 1 teaspoon salt, 1/2 teaspoon black pepper, paprika, garlic powder, and onion powder.
2. **Prepare Egg Mixture:** In another shallow dish, whisk together the eggs and buttermilk.

3. Bread the Steaks:

1. **Dredge:** Dip each steak into the flour mixture, coating both sides. Shake off excess flour.
2. **Dip in Egg Mixture:** Next, dip the steak into the egg mixture, letting any excess drip off.
3. **Coat Again:** Return the steak to the flour mixture for a second coating, pressing lightly to adhere. Shake off excess flour.

4. Fry the Steaks:

1. **Heat Oil:** In a large skillet, heat about 1/4 inch of vegetable oil over medium-high heat. The oil should be hot but not smoking, around 350°F (175°C).

2. **Fry Steaks:** Carefully place the breaded steaks in the hot oil. Fry for about 3-4 minutes per side, or until golden brown and crispy. Adjust the heat as needed to avoid burning.
3. **Drain:** Remove the steaks from the skillet and place them on a paper towel-lined plate to drain.

5. Make the Gravy:

1. **Make a Roux:** In the same skillet with the leftover oil and drippings, sprinkle 3 tablespoons of flour. Cook over medium heat, stirring constantly, for about 2 minutes to form a roux.
2. **Add Liquids:** Gradually whisk in 2 cups of milk and 1/2 cup of chicken broth, making sure to smooth out any lumps. Continue to cook, stirring frequently, until the gravy thickens and reaches the desired consistency. This should take about 5-7 minutes.
3. **Season:** Season the gravy with salt and black pepper to taste. If the gravy is too thick, you can add a bit more milk to thin it out.

6. Serve:

1. **Serve Warm:** Serve the Chicken Fried Steaks with the gravy poured over the top. They are delicious with mashed potatoes, green beans, or biscuits.

Tips:

- **Oil Temperature:** Keep an eye on the oil temperature to ensure the steaks cook evenly and become crispy without burning.
- **Gravy Variations:** For extra flavor, you can add a splash of hot sauce or a pinch of cayenne pepper to the gravy.

Enjoy your hearty and comforting Chicken Fried Steak!

Southern Corn Chowder

Ingredients:

- 4 cups fresh corn kernels (from about 6-8 ears of corn) or 3 cups frozen corn
- 4 slices bacon, diced
- 1 medium onion, chopped
- 2 cloves garlic, minced
- 1 medium bell pepper, chopped (red or green)
- 2 medium potatoes, peeled and diced
- 1 cup celery, chopped
- 4 cups chicken broth (or vegetable broth)
- 1 cup whole milk
- 1 cup heavy cream
- 1 teaspoon dried thyme
- 1/2 teaspoon paprika
- 1/2 teaspoon salt (or to taste)
- 1/4 teaspoon black pepper (or to taste)
- 1/4 cup all-purpose flour (optional, for thickening)
- Chopped fresh parsley or chives (for garnish)

Instructions:

1. Cook the Bacon:

1. **Render Bacon:** In a large pot or Dutch oven, cook the diced bacon over medium heat until crispy. Remove the bacon with a slotted spoon and set aside on paper towels. Leave about 1-2 tablespoons of bacon drippings in the pot.

2. Sauté Vegetables:

1. **Cook Vegetables:** In the same pot with the bacon drippings, add the chopped onion, garlic, and bell pepper. Sauté over medium heat until the vegetables are softened, about 5 minutes.
2. **Add Potatoes and Celery:** Stir in the diced potatoes and chopped celery. Cook for another 5 minutes.

3. Add Corn and Broth:

1. **Add Corn and Broth:** Add the corn kernels and pour in the chicken broth. Stir to combine.
2. **Simmer:** Bring the mixture to a boil, then reduce heat and let simmer for about 15-20 minutes, or until the potatoes are tender.

4. Make the Chowder Creamy:

1. **Add Milk and Cream:** Stir in the milk and heavy cream. Cook for another 5 minutes, allowing the chowder to heat through and the flavors to meld.
2. **Thicken (Optional):** If you prefer a thicker chowder, you can whisk the flour with a little bit of milk to make a slurry, then stir it into the chowder. Simmer for an additional 5 minutes until thickened.

5. Season and Serve:

1. **Season:** Add dried thyme, paprika, salt, and black pepper to taste. Adjust seasoning if needed.
2. **Garnish:** Serve the chowder hot, garnished with the crispy bacon and chopped fresh parsley or chives.

Tips:

- **Corn Variations:** If using frozen corn, you can use it directly without thawing. For added flavor, you can roast or grill fresh corn before adding it to the chowder.
- **Creaminess:** Adjust the amount of heavy cream and milk based on your preference for creaminess. For a lighter version, you can use all milk and omit the heavy cream.

Enjoy your delicious and comforting Southern Corn Chowder!

Biscuits and Sausage Gravy Casserole

Ingredients:

For the Casserole:

- 1 pound breakfast sausage (such as Jimmy Dean or your favorite brand)
- 1/2 cup chopped onion (optional)
- 1/4 cup all-purpose flour
- 2 cups whole milk
- 1/2 teaspoon garlic powder
- 1/2 teaspoon onion powder
- 1/4 teaspoon black pepper (or to taste)
- 1/4 teaspoon salt (or to taste)
- 1 can (16.3 ounces) refrigerated biscuit dough (like Pillsbury Grands!)
- 1 cup shredded cheddar cheese (optional)
- 1/4 teaspoon crushed red pepper flakes (optional, for a bit of heat)

For the Topping:

- 1/4 cup chopped fresh parsley or chives (optional, for garnish)

Instructions:

1. Prepare the Sausage Gravy:

1. **Cook Sausage:** In a large skillet over medium heat, cook the breakfast sausage until browned and crumbled, breaking it up with a spoon as it cooks. If using onion, add it to the skillet and cook until softened, about 5 minutes.
2. **Make Roux:** Sprinkle the flour over the cooked sausage and stir to combine. Cook for 1-2 minutes to form a roux.
3. **Add Milk:** Gradually whisk in the milk, making sure to smooth out any lumps. Continue to cook, stirring frequently, until the gravy thickens, about 5-7 minutes.
4. **Season:** Stir in garlic powder, onion powder, black pepper, and salt. Adjust seasoning to taste.

2. Prepare the Casserole:

1. **Preheat Oven:** Preheat your oven to 375°F (190°C).
2. **Prepare Biscuit Dough:** Open the can of biscuit dough and cut each biscuit into quarters.
3. **Assemble Casserole:** In a 9x13-inch baking dish, spread the biscuit pieces evenly. Pour the sausage gravy over the biscuit pieces, spreading it out evenly. If using cheese, sprinkle the shredded cheddar cheese on top of the gravy.

4. **Add Red Pepper Flakes:** If desired, sprinkle crushed red pepper flakes over the top for a bit of heat.

3. Bake the Casserole:

1. **Bake:** Bake in the preheated oven for 25-30 minutes, or until the biscuits are cooked through and golden brown, and the gravy is bubbly.
2. **Cool Slightly:** Let the casserole cool for a few minutes before serving.

4. Garnish and Serve:

1. **Garnish:** If desired, garnish with chopped fresh parsley or chives.
2. **Serve:** Serve warm as a hearty breakfast, brunch, or even dinner.

Tips:

- **Gravy Thickness:** If the gravy thickens too much while standing, you can stir in a little more milk to loosen it before pouring over the biscuits.
- **Additions:** Feel free to mix in some cooked and crumbled bacon, sautéed mushrooms, or other vegetables into the sausage gravy for added flavor and texture.

Enjoy your delicious and comforting Biscuits and Sausage Gravy Casserole!

Sweet Tea

Ingredients:

- 6-8 tea bags (black tea, such as Lipton or Luzianne)
- 1 cup granulated sugar
- 4 cups boiling water
- 4 cups cold water
- Ice (for serving)
- Lemon slices or fresh mint (optional, for garnish)

Instructions:

1. Brew the Tea:

1. **Boil Water:** Bring 4 cups of water to a boil in a kettle or pot.
2. **Steep Tea Bags:** Place the tea bags in a heat-resistant pitcher. Pour the boiling water over the tea bags. Let steep for 5-7 minutes, depending on how strong you like your tea. Remove the tea bags and discard them.

2. Sweeten the Tea:

1. **Add Sugar:** While the tea is still warm, stir in 1 cup of granulated sugar until fully dissolved. Adjust the amount of sugar to taste if you prefer it sweeter or less sweet.

3. Cool the Tea:

1. **Add Cold Water:** Pour in 4 cups of cold water and stir to combine.
2. **Chill:** Let the tea cool to room temperature. You can also refrigerate it to chill faster if desired.

4. Serve:

1. **Serve Over Ice:** Fill glasses with ice and pour the chilled tea over the ice.
2. **Garnish (Optional):** Garnish with lemon slices or fresh mint if desired.

Tips:

- **Tea Strength:** If you prefer a stronger tea, you can let the tea bags steep for a bit longer or use an additional tea bag.
- **Sweetener Alternatives:** You can use alternatives like honey, agave syrup, or a sugar substitute if you prefer different sweeteners.
- **Flavor Variations:** For a twist, you can add a splash of fruit juice (like peach or raspberry) or a few sprigs of fresh herbs (like mint or basil) to the tea while it's brewing.

Enjoy your classic and refreshing Southern Sweet Tea!

Country Ham

Ingredients:

- 1 whole country ham (8-10 pounds, fully cured and smoked)
- 1/2 cup brown sugar
- 1/4 cup honey
- 1/4 cup Dijon mustard
- 1/4 cup apple cider vinegar or water
- 1/2 teaspoon ground black pepper
- 1/2 teaspoon ground cloves (optional)

Instructions:

1. Prepare the Ham:

1. **Soak the Ham:** If the ham is very salty (as country hams can be), soak it in cold water for 24-48 hours, changing the water every 8-12 hours to remove excess salt. This step is crucial to reduce the saltiness. If the ham is less salty, a shorter soaking time or skipping this step might be sufficient.
2. **Preheat Oven:** Preheat your oven to 325°F (165°C).

2. Cook the Ham:

1. **Remove Skin:** After soaking, remove the skin from the ham. You can leave a thin layer of fat for flavor.
2. **Score the Ham:** Score the surface of the ham in a diamond pattern with a sharp knife. This helps the glaze penetrate the meat.

3. Prepare the Glaze:

1. **Mix Glaze Ingredients:** In a small bowl, combine the brown sugar, honey, Dijon mustard, apple cider vinegar, black pepper, and ground cloves (if using). Stir until smooth.

4. Apply the Glaze:

1. **Brush with Glaze:** Place the ham in a roasting pan, brush it generously with the glaze, and reserve some glaze for basting later.
2. **Cover and Bake:** Cover the ham loosely with aluminum foil and bake in the preheated oven. Cooking time is typically about 15-20 minutes per pound. For an 8-10 pound ham, this will be approximately 2-3 hours.

5. Glaze and Caramelize:

1. **Baste and Uncover:** Every 30 minutes, baste the ham with the glaze. About 30 minutes before the ham is done, remove the foil to allow the ham to caramelize and develop a crispy, golden-brown crust.
2. **Check Temperature:** The ham is done when it reaches an internal temperature of 140°F (60°C).

6. Rest and Serve:

1. **Rest the Ham:** Remove the ham from the oven and let it rest for 15-20 minutes before slicing. This helps the juices redistribute and makes the ham easier to carve.
2. **Slice and Serve:** Slice the ham against the grain and serve warm or at room temperature.

Tips:

- **Glaze Variations:** For different flavors, you can experiment with adding ingredients to the glaze such as bourbon, pineapple juice, or brown mustard.
- **Leftovers:** Country ham can be used in a variety of dishes such as soups, sandwiches, or as a flavorful addition to beans and greens.

Enjoy your flavorful and traditional Southern Country Ham!

Sautéed Kale

Ingredients:

- 1 bunch kale (about 6-8 cups, washed and stems removed)
- 2 tablespoons olive oil
- 2-3 cloves garlic, minced
- 1/4 teaspoon red pepper flakes (optional, for a bit of heat)
- Salt and black pepper to taste
- 1 tablespoon lemon juice (optional, for brightness)
- 1/4 cup grated Parmesan cheese (optional, for a touch of umami)

Instructions:

1. Prepare the Kale:

1. **Wash and Dry:** Wash the kale thoroughly under cold water. Pat dry with paper towels or use a salad spinner to remove excess moisture.
2. **Remove Stems:** Remove the tough stems from the kale leaves. You can do this by holding the stem with one hand and stripping the leaves off with the other. Alternatively, you can cut the leaves from the stems.
3. **Chop:** Tear or chop the kale into bite-sized pieces.

2. Sauté the Kale:

1. **Heat Oil:** In a large skillet or sauté pan, heat 2 tablespoons of olive oil over medium heat.
2. **Add Garlic:** Add the minced garlic and red pepper flakes (if using). Sauté for about 1 minute, or until the garlic is fragrant but not browned.
3. **Add Kale:** Add the chopped kale to the skillet. It will likely seem like a lot, but it will cook down significantly.
4. **Sauté:** Cook the kale, stirring occasionally, for about 5-7 minutes, or until the kale is wilted and tender. If the kale starts to stick to the pan, you can add a splash of water or broth to help it cook.

3. Season and Serve:

1. **Season:** Season the sautéed kale with salt and black pepper to taste.
2. **Add Lemon Juice:** For added brightness, stir in 1 tablespoon of lemon juice, if desired.
3. **Add Parmesan (Optional):** Sprinkle grated Parmesan cheese over the kale just before serving for extra flavor.

Tips:

- **Flavor Variations:** You can add other seasonings or ingredients to customize the flavor. Try adding a splash of balsamic vinegar, a pinch of smoked paprika, or some toasted nuts for added texture.
- **Batch Cooking:** Sautéed kale is great for meal prep. It can be stored in an airtight container in the refrigerator for up to 4 days.

Enjoy your vibrant and nutritious sautéed kale!

Cucumber and Tomato Salad

Ingredients:

- 2 large cucumbers, peeled and sliced
- 2 cups cherry tomatoes or grape tomatoes, halved
- 1/4 red onion, thinly sliced
- 1/4 cup fresh parsley or basil, chopped
- 1 tablespoon olive oil
- 1 tablespoon red wine vinegar (or lemon juice)
- 1/2 teaspoon dried oregano (optional)
- Salt and black pepper to taste

Instructions:

1. Prepare the Vegetables:

1. **Slice Cucumbers:** Peel and slice the cucumbers into thin rounds. If the cucumbers have large seeds, you might want to scoop them out before slicing.
2. **Halve Tomatoes:** Cut the cherry or grape tomatoes in half.
3. **Slice Onion:** Thinly slice the red onion. If you prefer a milder flavor, you can soak the onion slices in cold water for a few minutes, then drain before adding to the salad.

2. Make the Dressing:

1. **Combine Ingredients:** In a small bowl, whisk together the olive oil, red wine vinegar (or lemon juice), dried oregano (if using), salt, and black pepper.

3. Assemble the Salad:

1. **Mix Vegetables:** In a large bowl, combine the cucumber slices, cherry tomatoes, and red onion.
2. **Add Dressing:** Pour the dressing over the vegetables and toss to coat evenly.
3. **Add Herbs:** Stir in the chopped fresh parsley or basil.

4. Chill and Serve:

1. **Chill:** For the best flavor, let the salad sit in the refrigerator for about 15-30 minutes before serving to allow the flavors to meld.
2. **Serve:** Serve chilled or at room temperature.

Tips:

- **Additions:** You can add other ingredients like feta cheese, olives, or avocado for extra flavor and texture.

- **Seasoning:** Adjust the seasoning to taste. You might want to add a little extra vinegar or a pinch of sugar if the tomatoes are very sweet or acidic.

Enjoy this crisp and vibrant Cucumber and Tomato Salad!

Fried Catfish Tacos

Ingredients:

For the Catfish:

- 1 pound catfish fillets, cut into strips
- 1 cup buttermilk
- 1 cup all-purpose flour
- 1 cup cornmeal
- 1 teaspoon paprika
- 1 teaspoon garlic powder
- 1 teaspoon onion powder
- 1/2 teaspoon cayenne pepper (optional, for heat)
- Salt and black pepper to taste
- Vegetable oil for frying

For the Slaw:

- 3 cups shredded cabbage (green or a mix of green and red)
- 1 cup shredded carrots
- 1/4 cup mayonnaise
- 2 tablespoons apple cider vinegar
- 1 tablespoon honey
- Salt and black pepper to taste

For the Sauce:

- 1/2 cup sour cream or Greek yogurt
- 2 tablespoons mayonnaise
- 1 tablespoon lime juice
- 1 teaspoon hot sauce (optional, for extra heat)
- 1/2 teaspoon garlic powder
- Salt and black pepper to taste

For Serving:

- 8 small flour or corn tortillas
- Lime wedges (for garnish)
- Fresh cilantro, chopped (for garnish)

Instructions:

1. Prepare the Catfish:

1. **Marinate:** Place the catfish strips in a bowl and cover with buttermilk. Let marinate for at least 30 minutes, or up to 2 hours in the refrigerator.
2. **Prepare Breading:** In a shallow dish, combine the flour, cornmeal, paprika, garlic powder, onion powder, cayenne pepper (if using), salt, and black pepper.
3. **Bread the Catfish:** Remove the catfish strips from the buttermilk, allowing excess to drip off. Dredge each strip in the flour mixture, coating evenly. Press lightly to adhere.
4. **Fry:** Heat about 1/2 inch of vegetable oil in a large skillet over medium-high heat. Once hot (around 350°F or 175°C), fry the catfish strips in batches, cooking for about 3-4 minutes per side, or until golden brown and crispy. Remove from the skillet and drain on paper towels.

2. Prepare the Slaw:

1. **Mix Slaw Ingredients:** In a large bowl, combine the shredded cabbage and carrots. In a separate small bowl, whisk together the mayonnaise, apple cider vinegar, honey, salt, and black pepper.
2. **Combine:** Pour the dressing over the cabbage and carrots and toss to coat. Adjust seasoning as needed.

3. Prepare the Sauce:

1. **Mix Sauce Ingredients:** In a small bowl, mix together the sour cream or Greek yogurt, mayonnaise, lime juice, hot sauce (if using), garlic powder, salt, and black pepper.

4. Assemble the Tacos:

1. **Warm Tortillas:** Warm the tortillas in a dry skillet or microwave until pliable.
2. **Assemble:** Spread a spoonful of sauce on each tortilla. Add a few pieces of fried catfish, top with slaw, and garnish with fresh cilantro. Serve with lime wedges on the side for squeezing over the tacos.

Tips:

- **Oil Temperature:** Keep an eye on the oil temperature to ensure the catfish cooks evenly and doesn't burn. Adjust the heat as needed.
- **Slaw Variations:** Add extra ingredients to the slaw like sliced radishes or jalapeños for more flavor.
- **Sauce Variations:** For a different twist, you can add a touch of honey or a dash of smoked paprika to the sauce.

Enjoy your crispy and flavorful Fried Catfish Tacos!

Smothered Pork Chops

Ingredients:

- 4 bone-in pork chops (about 1-inch thick)
- Salt and black pepper to taste
- 1/2 cup all-purpose flour
- 2 tablespoons vegetable oil or butter
- 1 large onion, thinly sliced
- 2 cloves garlic, minced
- 2 cups chicken broth (or pork broth)
- 1 teaspoon dried thyme
- 1 teaspoon paprika
- 1/2 teaspoon garlic powder
- 1/2 teaspoon onion powder
- 1 bay leaf
- 1 tablespoon Worcestershire sauce (optional)
- 1/2 cup heavy cream (optional, for extra richness)
- Fresh parsley, chopped (for garnish, optional)

Instructions:

1. Prepare the Pork Chops:

1. **Season:** Season the pork chops generously with salt and black pepper.
2. **Dredge in Flour:** Place the flour in a shallow dish. Dredge each pork chop in the flour, shaking off any excess.

2. Sear the Pork Chops:

1. **Heat Oil:** In a large skillet or Dutch oven, heat the vegetable oil or butter over medium-high heat.
2. **Sear Chops:** Add the pork chops and sear for about 3-4 minutes per side, or until golden brown. Remove the pork chops from the skillet and set aside.

3. Make the Onion Gravy:

1. **Sauté Onions:** In the same skillet, add the sliced onions and cook over medium heat until they begin to soften, about 5 minutes.
2. **Add Garlic:** Add the minced garlic and cook for an additional 1 minute, stirring frequently.
3. **Deglaze Pan:** Pour in a small amount of chicken broth to deglaze the pan, scraping up any browned bits from the bottom of the skillet.
4. **Add Broth and Seasonings:** Add the remaining chicken broth, dried thyme, paprika, garlic powder, onion powder, and bay leaf. Stir to combine.

4. Smother the Pork Chops:

1. **Return Pork Chops:** Return the seared pork chops to the skillet, placing them on top of the onions and gravy.
2. **Simmer:** Reduce heat to low, cover, and simmer for 20-25 minutes, or until the pork chops are tender and cooked through (internal temperature should be 145°F or 63°C).

5. Finish the Gravy (Optional):

1. **Add Cream:** If you prefer a richer gravy, stir in the heavy cream during the last 5 minutes of cooking. Adjust seasoning with additional salt and pepper if needed.

6. Serve:

1. **Garnish:** Garnish with chopped fresh parsley, if desired.
2. **Serve:** Serve the smothered pork chops with mashed potatoes, rice, or biscuits to soak up the delicious gravy.

Tips:

- **Tender Chops:** If you find the pork chops are not as tender as you'd like, you can simmer them for a bit longer in the gravy.
- **Thickening Gravy:** If the gravy needs thickening, you can make a slurry by mixing 1-2 tablespoons of flour with a little cold water, then stir it into the gravy and cook for a few more minutes.
- **Flavor Variations:** Add sliced mushrooms or bell peppers to the onions for added flavor and texture.

Enjoy your flavorful and comforting Smothered Pork Chops!

Sloppy Joes

Ingredients:

- 1 pound ground beef
- 1 medium onion, finely chopped
- 1 bell pepper, finely chopped (red or green)
- 2 cloves garlic, minced
- 1 cup ketchup
- 1/4 cup tomato paste
- 2 tablespoons Worcestershire sauce
- 2 tablespoons brown sugar
- 1 tablespoon apple cider vinegar
- 1 teaspoon Dijon mustard
- 1/2 teaspoon smoked paprika
- 1/4 teaspoon cayenne pepper (optional, for heat)
- Salt and black pepper to taste
- 4-6 hamburger buns
- Pickles or coleslaw (optional, for serving)

Instructions:

1. Cook the Ground Beef:

1. **Brown Beef:** In a large skillet over medium-high heat, cook the ground beef, breaking it up with a spoon, until browned and cooked through, about 5-7 minutes. Drain any excess fat.

2. Add Vegetables:

1. **Sauté Onions and Peppers:** Add the finely chopped onion and bell pepper to the skillet with the beef. Cook until the vegetables are softened, about 5 minutes.
2. **Add Garlic:** Stir in the minced garlic and cook for an additional 1 minute, until fragrant.

3. Make the Sauce:

1. **Combine Ingredients:** Stir in the ketchup, tomato paste, Worcestershire sauce, brown sugar, apple cider vinegar, Dijon mustard, smoked paprika, and cayenne pepper (if using).
2. **Simmer:** Bring the mixture to a simmer, then reduce heat to low. Cook for about 10-15 minutes, or until the sauce has thickened and the flavors are well combined. Stir occasionally. Adjust seasoning with salt and black pepper to taste.

4. Prepare the Buns:

1. **Toast Buns (Optional):** If desired, lightly toast the hamburger buns under a broiler or in a toaster for extra texture.

5. Serve:

1. **Assemble:** Spoon the sloppy joe mixture onto the bottom half of each bun. Top with the other half of the bun.
2. **Garnish:** Serve with pickles or coleslaw if desired.

Tips:

- **Make Ahead:** The sloppy joe mixture can be made ahead of time and stored in the refrigerator for up to 3 days or frozen for up to 3 months. Reheat before serving.
- **Spicy Variation:** Add hot sauce or increase the cayenne pepper if you like your sloppy joes spicier.
- **Vegetable Add-ins:** You can add other vegetables like diced mushrooms or zucchini for extra nutrition and flavor.

Enjoy your hearty and flavorful Sloppy Joes!

Corn Pudding

Ingredients:

- 1 can (15 ounces) creamed corn
- 1 can (15 ounces) whole kernel corn, drained
- 1 cup sour cream
- 1/2 cup melted butter
- 1/4 cup granulated sugar
- 1/4 cup all-purpose flour
- 3 large eggs
- 1/2 teaspoon salt
- 1/2 teaspoon black pepper
- 1/2 teaspoon baking powder (optional, for extra fluffiness)
- 1 cup shredded cheddar cheese (optional, for added flavor)

Instructions:

1. Preheat Oven:

1. **Preheat Oven:** Preheat your oven to 350°F (175°C).

2. Prepare the Mixture:

1. **Mix Ingredients:** In a large bowl, combine the creamed corn, drained whole kernel corn, sour cream, melted butter, sugar, flour, eggs, salt, and black pepper. Stir until well combined. If using, mix in the shredded cheddar cheese.

3. Bake:

1. **Grease Dish:** Grease a 2-quart baking dish or casserole dish with butter or non-stick spray.
2. **Pour Mixture:** Pour the corn mixture into the prepared dish, spreading it evenly.
3. **Bake:** Bake in the preheated oven for 45-50 minutes, or until the top is golden brown and the pudding is set in the middle. A knife inserted into the center should come out clean.

4. Cool and Serve:

1. **Cool Slightly:** Let the corn pudding cool for a few minutes before serving. This allows it to set further and makes it easier to cut into squares.

Tips:

- **Texture Variations:** For a slightly different texture, you can add a cup of crushed or chopped crackers to the mixture or top with crushed crackers before baking.
- **Add-ins:** Consider adding cooked bacon, green onions, or diced jalapeños for extra flavor.
- **Make-Ahead:** Corn pudding can be made ahead of time. Prepare the dish up to a day in advance, cover, and refrigerate. Reheat in the oven before serving.

Enjoy your creamy and comforting Corn Pudding!

Broccoli and Cheese Casserole

Ingredients:

- 4 cups fresh broccoli florets (or about 1 pound frozen broccoli florets, thawed and drained)
- 1 cup shredded cheddar cheese (plus extra for topping)
- 1/2 cup grated Parmesan cheese
- 1 cup mayonnaise
- 1/2 cup sour cream
- 1 can (10.5 ounces) cream of mushroom soup (or cream of chicken soup)
- 1 small onion, finely chopped
- 1/2 teaspoon garlic powder
- 1/2 teaspoon onion powder
- Salt and black pepper to taste
- 1/2 cup crushed Ritz crackers or breadcrumbs (for topping)
- 2 tablespoons melted butter (for topping)

Instructions:

1. Preheat Oven:

1. **Preheat Oven:** Preheat your oven to 350°F (175°C).

2. Prepare the Broccoli:

1. **Cook Broccoli:** If using fresh broccoli, blanch it in boiling water for about 2-3 minutes until bright green and slightly tender. Drain and immediately transfer to an ice bath to stop the cooking process. Drain well and pat dry. If using frozen broccoli, make sure it is fully thawed and drained.

3. Prepare the Casserole Mixture:

1. **Combine Ingredients:** In a large bowl, mix together the shredded cheddar cheese, grated Parmesan cheese, mayonnaise, sour cream, cream of mushroom soup, chopped onion, garlic powder, onion powder, salt, and black pepper until well combined.
2. **Add Broccoli:** Gently fold the cooked broccoli into the mixture until evenly coated.

4. Assemble the Casserole:

1. **Grease Dish:** Grease a 9x13-inch baking dish or a similar-sized casserole dish.
2. **Pour Mixture:** Pour the broccoli and cheese mixture into the prepared dish and spread evenly.

5. Prepare the Topping:

1. **Cracker Topping:** In a small bowl, combine the crushed Ritz crackers or breadcrumbs with melted butter. Sprinkle this mixture evenly over the top of the casserole.

6. Bake:

1. **Bake:** Bake in the preheated oven for 30-35 minutes, or until the casserole is bubbly and the topping is golden brown.

7. Cool and Serve:

1. **Cool Slightly:** Let the casserole cool for a few minutes before serving. This helps it set and makes it easier to scoop.

Tips:

- **Cheese Varieties:** You can use different types of cheese, such as Monterey Jack or Gouda, for variation.
- **Add-ins:** For extra flavor, consider adding cooked bacon, diced ham, or a sprinkle of paprika.
- **Make-Ahead:** You can prepare the casserole a day in advance. Assemble it, cover, and refrigerate. Bake just before serving, adding a few extra minutes to the cooking time if needed.

Enjoy your creamy and cheesy Broccoli and Cheese Casserole!

Southern Shrimp Salad

Ingredients:

- 1 pound large shrimp, peeled and deveined
- 1 tablespoon olive oil
- 1/2 teaspoon smoked paprika
- 1/2 teaspoon garlic powder
- 1/4 teaspoon cayenne pepper (optional, for heat)
- Salt and black pepper to taste

For the Salad:

- 4 cups mixed greens or romaine lettuce
- 1 cup cherry tomatoes, halved
- 1/2 cucumber, sliced
- 1/4 red onion, thinly sliced
- 1/4 cup sliced black olives (optional)
- 1/4 cup crumbled feta cheese (optional)

For the Dressing:

- 1/2 cup mayonnaise
- 2 tablespoons Dijon mustard
- 1 tablespoon lemon juice
- 1 tablespoon chopped fresh dill (or 1 teaspoon dried dill)
- 1 teaspoon honey or sugar
- Salt and black pepper to taste

Instructions:

1. Prepare the Shrimp:

1. **Season Shrimp:** In a bowl, toss the shrimp with olive oil, smoked paprika, garlic powder, cayenne pepper (if using), salt, and black pepper.
2. **Cook Shrimp:** Heat a skillet over medium-high heat. Add the seasoned shrimp and cook for about 2-3 minutes per side, or until they are pink and opaque. Remove from heat and let cool slightly.

2. Prepare the Salad:

1. **Assemble Salad:** In a large bowl, toss together the mixed greens, cherry tomatoes, cucumber, red onion, and black olives (if using).
2. **Add Feta:** If using feta cheese, sprinkle it over the salad.

3. Make the Dressing:

1. **Combine Ingredients:** In a small bowl, whisk together the mayonnaise, Dijon mustard, lemon juice, chopped dill, and honey or sugar. Season with salt and black pepper to taste.

4. Combine and Serve:

1. **Add Shrimp:** Top the salad with the cooked shrimp.
2. **Dress Salad:** Drizzle the dressing over the salad or serve it on the side.
3. **Toss:** Toss gently to combine, or serve the shrimp and dressing on top of the salad.

Tips:

- **Make-Ahead:** The shrimp and dressing can be prepared a day in advance. Store separately and combine just before serving to keep the salad fresh.
- **Add-ins:** Feel free to add other ingredients like avocado, corn, or bell peppers for additional flavor and texture.
- **Serving:** This salad is delicious on its own or served with crusty bread or as a topping for a grain bowl.

Enjoy your refreshing and flavorful Southern Shrimp Salad!

Cajun Dirty Rice

Ingredients:

- 1 pound ground pork (or a mix of pork and beef)
- 1/2 pound chicken livers, trimmed and chopped (optional, for authentic flavor)
- 1 tablespoon vegetable oil
- 1 large onion, finely chopped
- 1 bell pepper, finely chopped (red or green)
- 2 cloves garlic, minced
- 2 celery stalks, finely chopped
- 1 cup long-grain white rice
- 2 cups chicken broth
- 1 tablespoon Cajun seasoning (store-bought or homemade)
- 1 teaspoon dried thyme
- 1/2 teaspoon paprika
- 1/4 teaspoon cayenne pepper (optional, for extra heat)
- Salt and black pepper to taste
- 2 green onions, sliced (for garnish)
- Fresh parsley, chopped (for garnish)

Instructions:

1. Cook the Meat:

1. **Brown Meat:** In a large skillet or Dutch oven, heat the vegetable oil over medium-high heat. Add the ground pork (and chicken livers if using) and cook, breaking it up with a spoon, until browned and cooked through. Remove excess fat if necessary.

2. Add Vegetables:

1. **Sauté Vegetables:** Add the chopped onion, bell pepper, celery, and garlic to the skillet with the meat. Cook, stirring occasionally, until the vegetables are softened, about 5 minutes.

3. Add Rice and Seasonings:

1. **Stir in Rice:** Add the rice to the skillet and stir to combine with the meat and vegetables.
2. **Add Broth and Spices:** Pour in the chicken broth and stir in the Cajun seasoning, dried thyme, paprika, cayenne pepper (if using), salt, and black pepper. Stir to combine.

4. Simmer:

1. **Cook Rice:** Bring the mixture to a boil. Reduce heat to low, cover, and simmer for about 20-25 minutes, or until the rice is tender and the liquid is absorbed. Check occasionally and add a bit more broth if needed to prevent the rice from sticking.

5. Finish and Garnish:

1. **Fluff Rice:** Once the rice is cooked, remove from heat and let it sit covered for 5 minutes. Fluff the rice with a fork.
2. **Garnish:** Stir in the sliced green onions and chopped parsley before serving.

Tips:

- **Homemade Cajun Seasoning:** If you want to make your own Cajun seasoning, combine paprika, garlic powder, onion powder, dried oregano, dried thyme, cayenne pepper, salt, and black pepper.
- **Texture:** For a slightly different texture, you can use a mix of brown rice or other whole grains.
- **Additions:** You can add additional ingredients like cooked sausage, shrimp, or diced tomatoes to enhance the dish.

Enjoy your flavorful and comforting Cajun Dirty Rice!

Hot Water Cornbread

Ingredients:

- 1 cup cornmeal (yellow or white)
- 1/2 cup all-purpose flour
- 1 teaspoon baking powder
- 1/2 teaspoon salt
- 1 cup hot water
- 2 tablespoons sugar (optional, for a touch of sweetness)
- 2 tablespoons vegetable oil or melted butter (for added richness)
- Additional vegetable oil for frying

Instructions:

1. Prepare the Batter:

1. **Mix Dry Ingredients:** In a large bowl, combine the cornmeal, flour, baking powder, salt, and sugar (if using).
2. **Add Wet Ingredients:** Slowly pour in the hot water while stirring the mixture until smooth. Add the vegetable oil or melted butter and mix until well combined. The batter should be thick but pourable.

2. Heat the Oil:

1. **Heat Skillet:** In a large skillet or cast-iron pan, heat about 1/4 inch of vegetable oil over medium-high heat. The oil should be hot but not smoking; a drop of batter should sizzle when added.

3. Cook the Cornbread:

1. **Fry:** Drop spoonfuls of batter (about 2-3 tablespoons per piece) into the hot oil, flattening them slightly with the back of the spoon. Fry the cornbread until golden brown and crispy on both sides, about 2-3 minutes per side.
2. **Drain:** Remove the cornbread from the skillet and place them on paper towels to drain excess oil.

4. Serve:

1. **Enjoy:** Serve the hot water cornbread warm. It's great on its own or with butter, honey, or your favorite savory dishes.

Tips:

- **Texture:** If the batter is too thick, you can add a bit more hot water to reach the desired consistency.
- **Seasoning:** Feel free to add extra flavorings like finely chopped onions, jalapeños, or herbs to the batter.
- **Frying:** Make sure the oil is hot enough before adding the batter to get a crispy crust. Test with a small drop of batter to check.

Enjoy your crispy and delicious Hot Water Cornbread!

Apple Butter

Ingredients:

- 4 pounds apples (about 8 medium apples; a mix of sweet and tart varieties works well)
- 1 cup apple cider or apple juice
- 1 cup granulated sugar
- 1 cup packed brown sugar
- 1 tablespoon ground cinnamon
- 1/2 teaspoon ground cloves
- 1/2 teaspoon ground allspice
- 1/4 teaspoon ground nutmeg
- 1/4 teaspoon salt
- 2 tablespoons lemon juice

Instructions:

1. Prepare the Apples:

1. **Peel, Core, and Chop:** Peel, core, and cut the apples into chunks. They don't need to be perfect as they will be cooked down and pureed.

2. Cook the Apples:

1. **Combine Ingredients:** Place the apple chunks in a large slow cooker or a heavy-bottomed pot. Add the apple cider or apple juice.
2. **Cook:**
   - **Slow Cooker:** Cook on low for 6-8 hours, or until the apples are very soft and can be easily mashed.
   - **Stovetop:** Cook over medium heat, stirring occasionally, for about 1.5-2 hours, or until the apples are soft.

3. Puree the Apples:

1. **Blend:** Use an immersion blender to puree the apples directly in the slow cooker or pot. Alternatively, transfer the apples in batches to a blender or food processor and blend until smooth.

4. Add Spices and Sweeteners:

1. **Mix in Spices and Sugars:** Stir in the granulated sugar, brown sugar, cinnamon, cloves, allspice, nutmeg, salt, and lemon juice. Mix well.

5. Continue Cooking:

1. **Cook Down:**

- **Slow Cooker:** Continue cooking on low for an additional 2-3 hours, or until the mixture is thick and spreadable.
- **Stovetop:** Continue cooking over low heat, stirring frequently, for 30-60 minutes, or until the apple butter reaches your desired consistency.

6. Check for Consistency:

1. **Test:** To check the thickness, place a small spoonful of apple butter on a plate and let it cool. Run your finger through the middle; if it holds its shape and doesn't run, it's ready.

7. Store the Apple Butter:

1. **Jar and Seal:**
   - **Hot Pack:** Pour the hot apple butter into sterilized jars, leaving 1/4-inch headspace. Wipe the rims with a clean, damp cloth and seal with lids and bands.
   - **Refrigerate or Process:**
     - For immediate use, let the jars cool to room temperature and store in the refrigerator.
     - For longer storage, process the jars in a boiling water bath for 5-10 minutes (adjust based on altitude).

Tips:

- **Sweetness:** Adjust the amount of sugar to your taste. You can reduce the sugar or use alternative sweeteners if desired.
- **Spices:** Feel free to adjust the spices based on your preferences. Adding a bit of ginger or cardamom can also enhance the flavor.
- **Storage:** Properly canned apple butter can be stored in a cool, dark place for up to a year.

Enjoy your homemade Apple Butter on toast, pancakes, or as a delicious spread for various dishes!

Poppy Seed Chicken

Ingredients:

- 4 cups cooked chicken, shredded or cubed (about 3-4 chicken breasts)
- 1 can (10.5 ounces) cream of chicken soup
- 1 cup sour cream
- 1/2 cup mayonnaise
- 2 tablespoons poppy seeds
- 1/2 teaspoon garlic powder
- 1/2 teaspoon onion powder
- 1/2 teaspoon dried parsley flakes
- 1 cup crushed Ritz crackers or breadcrumbs (for topping)
- 2 tablespoons melted butter (for topping)
- Salt and black pepper to taste

Instructions:

1. Preheat Oven:

1. **Preheat Oven:** Preheat your oven to 350°F (175°C).

2. Prepare the Chicken Mixture:

1. **Combine Ingredients:** In a large bowl, mix together the cream of chicken soup, sour cream, mayonnaise, poppy seeds, garlic powder, onion powder, dried parsley, salt, and black pepper.
2. **Add Chicken:** Fold in the cooked chicken until well coated with the mixture.

3. Assemble the Casserole:

1. **Grease Dish:** Grease a 9x13-inch baking dish or a similar-sized casserole dish.
2. **Pour Mixture:** Pour the chicken mixture into the prepared dish and spread it evenly.

4. Prepare the Topping:

1. **Mix Topping:** In a small bowl, combine the crushed Ritz crackers or breadcrumbs with melted butter. Sprinkle this mixture evenly over the top of the chicken mixture.

5. Bake:

1. **Bake:** Bake in the preheated oven for 30-35 minutes, or until the top is golden brown and the casserole is bubbly.

6. Serve:

1. **Cool Slightly:** Let the casserole cool for a few minutes before serving. This helps it set and makes it easier to serve.

Tips:

- **Chicken:** This recipe is a great way to use leftover cooked chicken or rotisserie chicken. You can also use chicken thighs or legs for added flavor.
- **Cream Soup:** If you prefer a lighter version, you can use a low-fat cream of chicken soup.
- **Add-ins:** Feel free to add vegetables like peas or mushrooms to the chicken mixture for added texture and flavor.
- **Make-Ahead:** You can assemble the casserole a day in advance. Cover and refrigerate it, then bake it just before serving, adding a few extra minutes to the cooking time if needed.

Enjoy your creamy and delicious Poppy Seed Chicken casserole!

Southern Cornbread Dressing

Ingredients:

For the Cornbread:

- 1 cup cornmeal
- 1 cup all-purpose flour
- 1/4 cup granulated sugar
- 1 tablespoon baking powder
- 1/2 teaspoon salt
- 1 cup milk
- 2 large eggs
- 1/4 cup melted butter or vegetable oil

For the Dressing:

- 1/2 cup butter (1 stick)
- 1 large onion, finely chopped
- 2 celery stalks, finely chopped
- 3-4 cloves garlic, minced
- 1 tablespoon fresh sage, chopped (or 1 teaspoon dried sage)
- 1 tablespoon fresh thyme, chopped (or 1 teaspoon dried thyme)
- 4 cups crumbled cornbread (from the recipe above)
- 2-3 cups chicken or vegetable broth (adjust for desired moisture level)
- 1 large egg, beaten
- Salt and black pepper to taste

Instructions:

1. Prepare the Cornbread:

1. **Preheat Oven:** Preheat your oven to 425°F (220°C).
2. **Mix Dry Ingredients:** In a large bowl, combine cornmeal, flour, sugar, baking powder, and salt.
3. **Mix Wet Ingredients:** In another bowl, whisk together milk, eggs, and melted butter or oil.
4. **Combine:** Pour the wet ingredients into the dry ingredients and stir until just combined.
5. **Bake:** Pour the batter into a greased 8x8-inch baking dish or similar-sized pan. Bake for 20-25 minutes, or until the cornbread is golden brown and a toothpick inserted in the center comes out clean. Let it cool completely before crumbling for the dressing.

2. Prepare the Dressing:

1. **Sauté Vegetables:** In a large skillet, melt the butter over medium heat. Add the chopped onion, celery, and garlic. Sauté until the vegetables are softened, about 5-7 minutes.
2. **Add Herbs:** Stir in the chopped sage and thyme, cooking for another minute until fragrant.
3. **Combine Ingredients:** In a large bowl, combine the crumbled cornbread with the sautéed vegetables. Stir in the beaten egg and 2 cups of broth. Mix until well combined. Add more broth if needed to reach your desired consistency; the mixture should be moist but not soupy. Season with salt and black pepper to taste.

3. Bake the Dressing:

1. **Transfer to Dish:** Transfer the dressing mixture to a greased 9x13-inch baking dish or a similar-sized casserole dish.
2. **Bake:** Bake in the preheated oven at 350°F (175°C) for 30-35 minutes, or until the top is golden brown and the dressing is heated through.

4. Serve:

1. **Cool Slightly:** Let the dressing cool for a few minutes before serving. This allows it to set and makes it easier to serve.

Tips:

- **Cornbread:** Make the cornbread a day ahead of time for better texture in the dressing.
- **Add-ins:** For extra flavor, you can add cooked sausage, chopped apples, or dried cranberries.
- **Moisture:** Adjust the amount of broth based on how moist or dry you prefer your dressing. It should be moist but not overly wet before baking.

Enjoy your Southern Cornbread Dressing with your favorite holiday meals or as a comforting side dish any time of year!

Grits Casserole

Ingredients:

- 1 cup stone-ground grits
- 4 cups water or chicken broth
- 1/2 teaspoon salt
- 1/4 teaspoon black pepper
- 1/4 teaspoon garlic powder
- 2 cups shredded sharp cheddar cheese
- 1/2 cup grated Parmesan cheese
- 2 large eggs, beaten
- 1/2 cup milk or cream
- 1/4 cup butter, melted
- 1 cup cooked and crumbled sausage or bacon (optional)
- 1/2 cup finely chopped green onions (optional)
- 1/2 cup diced bell peppers (optional)
- 1/4 cup chopped fresh parsley (optional, for garnish)

Instructions:

1. Cook the Grits:

1. **Boil Liquid:** In a medium saucepan, bring the water or chicken broth to a boil.
2. **Add Grits:** Stir in the grits and salt. Reduce heat to low and cover. Cook, stirring occasionally, until the grits are thick and tender, about 20-25 minutes.

2. Prepare the Grits Mixture:

1. **Preheat Oven:** Preheat your oven to 350°F (175°C).
2. **Mix Ingredients:** In a large bowl, combine the cooked grits with the shredded cheddar cheese, grated Parmesan cheese, beaten eggs, milk or cream, melted butter, black pepper, and garlic powder. Stir in any optional ingredients like cooked sausage, bacon, green onions, or bell peppers if using.

3. Assemble the Casserole:

1. **Grease Dish:** Grease a 9x13-inch baking dish or a similar-sized casserole dish.
2. **Pour Mixture:** Pour the grits mixture into the prepared dish and spread it evenly.

4. Bake:

1. **Bake:** Bake in the preheated oven for 30-40 minutes, or until the casserole is set and the top is golden brown.

5. Garnish and Serve:

1. **Cool Slightly:** Let the casserole cool for a few minutes before serving.
2. **Garnish:** Garnish with chopped fresh parsley if desired.

Tips:

- **Texture:** For a creamier texture, you can add more milk or cream. For a firmer casserole, reduce the amount of liquid.
- **Cheese Varieties:** Feel free to use different types of cheese such as Monterey Jack or Gouda for a different flavor profile.
- **Add-Ins:** Customize the casserole with additional ingredients like sautéed mushrooms, spinach, or diced tomatoes for added flavor and texture.

Enjoy your creamy and cheesy Grits Casserole!

Hoppin' John

Ingredients:

- 1 pound dried black-eyed peas (or 3 cups cooked or canned black-eyed peas, drained)
- 4 cups water (if using dried peas)
- 1/2 pound bacon, diced (or 1 smoked ham hock)
- 1 large onion, chopped
- 1 bell pepper, chopped (green or red)
- 2 cloves garlic, minced
- 2 cups long-grain white rice
- 1 can (14.5 ounces) diced tomatoes, undrained
- 1 teaspoon dried thyme
- 1/2 teaspoon paprika
- 1/4 teaspoon cayenne pepper (optional, for heat)
- 1 bay leaf
- 2 cups chicken broth
- Salt and black pepper to taste
- 2 green onions, sliced (for garnish)
- Fresh parsley, chopped (for garnish)

Instructions:

1. Prepare the Black-Eyed Peas:

1. **Soak Peas (if using dried):** Rinse the dried peas and soak them overnight in plenty of water. Alternatively, you can use the quick soak method: cover peas with water, bring to a boil, then remove from heat and let sit for 1 hour. Drain and rinse before using.

2. Cook the Bacon (or Ham Hock):

1. **Cook Bacon:** In a large pot or Dutch oven, cook the diced bacon over medium heat until crispy. Remove the bacon with a slotted spoon and set aside, leaving the rendered fat in the pot. If using a ham hock, add it to the pot without cooking.

3. Sauté Vegetables:

1. **Sauté:** Add the chopped onion, bell pepper, and garlic to the pot with the bacon fat. Sauté over medium heat until the vegetables are softened, about 5-7 minutes.

4. Combine Ingredients:

1. **Add Peas and Rice:** Add the soaked and drained black-eyed peas (or cooked/canned peas) to the pot. Stir in the rice, diced tomatoes, dried thyme, paprika, cayenne pepper (if using), bay leaf, and chicken broth.

2. **Add Bacon:** Return the cooked bacon to the pot if using, or add the smoked ham hock.

5. Cook:

1. **Simmer:** Bring the mixture to a boil. Reduce heat to low, cover, and simmer for about 45 minutes to 1 hour (if using dried peas), or until the peas are tender and the rice is cooked. If using canned peas, cook for about 20-25 minutes.
2. **Check Consistency:** Check occasionally and add more broth or water if necessary to keep the dish from becoming too dry.

6. Season and Garnish:

1. **Season:** Taste and adjust seasoning with salt and black pepper.
2. **Remove Bay Leaf:** Discard the bay leaf before serving.
3. **Garnish:** Garnish with sliced green onions and chopped parsley if desired.

Tips:

- **Peas:** If you're using canned black-eyed peas, be sure to drain and rinse them to reduce the sodium content.
- **Texture:** If you prefer a thicker consistency, you can mash some of the peas against the side of the pot with a spoon.
- **Additions:** Feel free to add other ingredients like hot sauce, chopped tomatoes, or cooked sausage for extra flavor.

Enjoy your traditional Hoppin' John, a hearty and flavorful dish that's sure to bring a taste of Southern comfort to your table!

Boiled Peanuts

Ingredients:

- 2 pounds raw peanuts (in the shell)
- 1/2 cup salt
- 1 tablespoon Old Bay seasoning (optional, for extra flavor)
- 1 tablespoon crushed red pepper flakes (optional, for heat)
- 1 bay leaf (optional)
- 2-3 cloves garlic, crushed (optional)
- Water (enough to cover the peanuts)

Instructions:

1. Prepare the Peanuts:

1. **Rinse Peanuts:** Rinse the raw peanuts under cold water to remove any dirt and debris.

2. Cook the Peanuts:

1. **Boil Water:** In a large pot, bring enough water to cover the peanuts to a boil.
2. **Add Seasonings:** Add the salt, Old Bay seasoning (if using), crushed red pepper flakes (if using), bay leaf, and garlic (if using) to the boiling water.
3. **Add Peanuts:** Add the peanuts to the pot. Stir to combine.

3. Simmer:

1. **Cook:** Reduce the heat to low and let the peanuts simmer, uncovered, for 2-4 hours. The cooking time will vary depending on the size and freshness of the peanuts. Stir occasionally and check for doneness.
2. **Test Peanuts:** To test for doneness, take a peanut out of the pot and let it cool slightly. The peanuts should be tender and easily chewable. They should not be too firm or crunchy.

4. Adjust Seasoning:

1. **Taste:** Taste the peanuts and adjust seasoning if needed. If they need more salt or spices, add them and simmer for an additional 10-15 minutes.

5. Serve:

1. **Drain:** Once the peanuts are tender, drain them from the cooking water.
2. **Cool:** Let the peanuts cool slightly before serving.

Tips:

- **Freshness:** Using fresh raw peanuts will yield the best results. If you can't find raw peanuts, make sure to use green peanuts if available, as they cook faster and are often used for boiling.
- **Seasoning Variations:** Feel free to experiment with other seasonings, such as smoked paprika, cayenne pepper, or even a splash of vinegar for a tangy twist.
- **Storage:** Boiled peanuts can be stored in the refrigerator for up to a week. They can also be frozen for longer storage. Reheat them in the microwave or on the stovetop with a little added water.

Enjoy your delicious boiled peanuts, a tasty and satisfying Southern treat!

Cherry Limeade

Ingredients:

- 1 cup freshly squeezed lime juice (about 6-8 limes)
- 1 cup cherry juice (or 1 cup fresh cherries, pitted and blended)
- 1/2 cup granulated sugar (adjust to taste)
- 4 cups cold water (or sparkling water for a fizzy version)
- Ice cubes
- Lime slices and fresh cherries (for garnish)

Instructions:

1. Make Cherry Juice (if using fresh cherries):

1. **Blend Cherries:** If using fresh cherries, pit and blend them until smooth. You can strain the mixture through a fine mesh sieve to remove any solids if you prefer a smoother juice.

2. Prepare the Limeade:

1. **Mix Lime Juice and Cherry Juice:** In a large pitcher, combine the freshly squeezed lime juice and cherry juice (or cherry puree).
2. **Add Sugar:** Stir in the granulated sugar until it is completely dissolved. If you prefer a less sweet drink, adjust the amount of sugar to taste.
3. **Add Water:** Pour in the cold water and stir well. If using sparkling water, add it just before serving to keep the fizz.

3. Serve:

1. **Chill:** Refrigerate the cherry limeade for at least 1-2 hours to chill.
2. **Serve Over Ice:** Fill glasses with ice cubes and pour the cherry limeade over the ice.
3. **Garnish:** Garnish with lime slices and fresh cherries if desired.

Tips:

- **Adjust Sweetness:** You can adjust the sweetness by adding more or less sugar, or use a sugar substitute if you prefer.
- **Sparkling Version:** For a fizzy cherry limeade, use sparkling water instead of still water. Add it just before serving to keep the bubbles.
- **Flavor Variations:** Add a splash of orange juice or a few mint leaves for a twist on the traditional flavor.

Enjoy your Cherry Limeade as a refreshing treat that's perfect for any occasion!

www.ingramcontent.com/pod-product-compliance
Lightning Source LLC
LaVergne TN
LVHW061942070526
838199LV00060B/3929